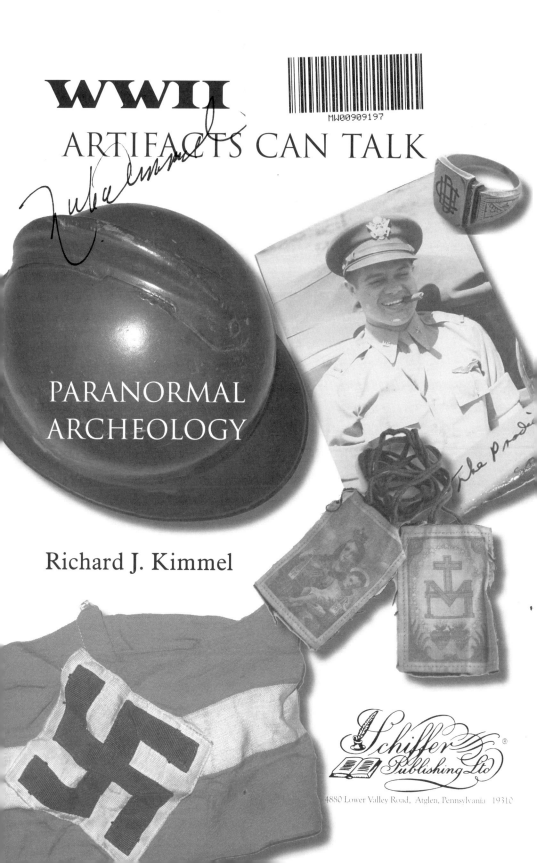

WWII
ARTIFACTS CAN TALK

PARANORMAL
ARCHEOLOGY

Richard J. Kimmel

Schiffer Publishing Ltd

4880 Lower Valley Road, Atglen, Pennsylvania 19310

Other Schiffer Books on Related Subjects:
Cape May Haunts: Elaine's Haunted Mansion and Other Eerie Beach Tales.
    D. P. Roseberry with Psychic Laurie Hull. ISBN: 9780764328213. $14.95
Ghosts of Hollywood II: Talking to Spirits.
    Marla Brooks. ISBN: 9780764329975. $14.99
Haunted Battlefields: Virginia's Civil War Ghosts.
    Beth Brown. ISBN: 9780764330575. $14.99
Philadelphia Haunts: Eastern State Penitentiary, Fort Mifflin, & Other Ghostly Sites.
    Katharine Sarro. ISBN: 9780764329876. $14.99

Schiffer Books are available at special discounts for bulk purchases for sales promotions or premiums. Special editions, including personalized covers, corporate imprints, and excerpts can be created in large quantities for special needs. For more information contact the publisher:

Schiffer Publishing Ltd.
4880 Lower Valley Road
Atglen, PA 19310
Phone: (610) 593-1777; Fax: (610) 593-2002
E-mail: Info@schifferbooks.com

For the largest selection of fine reference books on this and related subjects, please visit our web site at **www.schifferbooks.com** We are always looking for people to write books on new and related subjects. If you have an idea for a book please contact us at the above address.

This book may be purchased from the publisher. Include $5.00 for shipping. Please try your bookstore first. You may write for a free catalog.

In Europe, Schiffer books are distributed by
Bushwood Books
6 Marksbury Ave.
Kew Gardens
Surrey TW9 4JF England
Phone: 44 (0) 20 8392-8585; Fax: 44 (0) 20 8392-9876
E-mail: info@bushwoodbooks.co.uk
Website: www.bushwoodbooks.co.uk
Free postage in the U.K., Europe; air mail at cost.

Designed by Stephanie Daugherty
Type set in Bodoni Bd BT/Trajan Pro/Aldine 721 BT

ISBN: 978-0-7643-3159-6
Printed in the United States of America

CONTENTS

DEDICATION

Dedicated in loving memory to my grandfather, Otto Röthe – (12.30.1863 - 6.16.1947). During the early eighteen eighties, at the age of twenty-five, Otto served his country as a Lieutenant in the Royal Prussian Army. Leaving his hometown of Vandsburg Krs. Flatow, East Prussia, and immigrating to America, he began a more prosperous life. I will forever cherish the little time I had with him here in this realm.

Also, my never-ending gratitude to the veterans of all wars, both present and past, and to the spirits of those who may still walk among us.

ACKNOWLEDGMENTS

I wish to express my thanks to all who have contributed in some way with my book. Without them, some of the information and photographs would not have been possible. A special thank you to my family for their support during my writing of this book. Definitely without the help and patience from psychics Jane Doherty, Lisa Palandrano, and Maryanne Vasnelis, significant information surrounding the artifacts may never have surfaced. To a very special friend, Todd Bates, of Haunted Voices, who, in my opinion, is the guru of electronic voice phenomenon; without your support and always being there for me when I sought advice, I would be lost in the world of EVP's. A special thank you to my daughter, Karen Timper, friends, and associates Richard Wisenfelder and Gaspari Bua, for supplying the photos in several of my chapters, and to my son in law, Carl Labarbera Jr., for providing several artifacts from his collection. Special thanks to my friend, Don Boyle, the author of *SS Totenkopf H. Himmler Honor Ring 1933-1935*. A special thank you to my publisher and their support staff at Schiffer Books, and especially to my contract editor, Dinah Roseberry, for her help and patience with this senior citizen in bringing my book to fruition. Should I have left anyone out, my sincere apology, as it was not intentional, and once again my thanks to all.

FOREWORD

Artifacts are tangible remnants of the past that offer valuable information about the history of humanity. Without these historical gems, much knowledge of past conflicts and battles would be buried in time.

This book is a unique approach to history that takes the study of humanity to another level. It is a one-of-a-kind book that combines traditional research with paranormal methods. By using psychics, the author believes the artifact can provide its own story, opening a window in time. Thus, it could provide a deeper understanding of why and how our world has been shaped by conflict.

Richard Kimmel's photographs of his artifacts are visual treasure maps into the realities of World War II. He takes his artifacts, his military knowledge, and his pendulum to search for latent energy, his belief in psychic ability, and combines all of them to test the waters of a new frontier of research. Sometimes, he was shocked by the results of the research. Sometimes I quivered as I saw psychic images of the atrocities of war. The intense vibrations of energy emanating from some artifacts made me wonder if they are "haunted." Some artifacts needed to be "exorcised" in a bath of sea salt. Most artifacts haunted me with memories or nightmares after each hands-on session. Most of them made me squeamish as history came alive in my hands.

How is it possible for psychics to receive impressions? According to Quantum Theory, there are tiny bits of energy that come together and vibrate at a unique level for every person or thing. These "fingerprints of energy" mark anywhere you have been, anything closely associated to you, and even your thoughts have this energy. Psychics sense this energy and are then able to interpret it into images, feelings, and sounds.

Can artifacts talk? As you travel through these pages, you will discover your own answer. For me, the ghosts of these artifacts spoke loudly. History itself spoke to me and I am reminded of the many sacrifices these war-torn soldiers endured, I thank everyone who is now or who have ever served in the United States armed forces. I ask God to bless you and your family.

— Jane Doherty
Author of *Awakening the Mystic Gift*

ABOUT THE PSYCHICS

JANE DOHERTY

When author, psychic, and ghostbuster Jane Doherty lectured at the Breakfast Club, San Francisco's premiere high society club, she turned cautiously minded skeptics into soft-hearted, warm believers giddy with their newly found psychic possibilities. Jane is living proof that paranormal abilities can be acquired and with her first book, *Awakening the Mystic Gift: The Surprising Truth About What It Means to Be Psychic*, she wants to teach that message to the world.

A renowned psychic for more than fifteen years, giving tens of thousands of readings, Jane Doherty is the leading authority on psychic experiences. She provides individual guidance through private consultation, conducts ghost investigations and séances to communicate with the other side, and offers classes and workshops to those who are interested in discovering and developing their own psychic abilities. She was the star of a television series on a major network, called "Dead Tenants," which is now airing internationally.

Widely recognized and respected for her extraordinary skill and sensitivity, she has been featured on Fox Network News, CNN, The Today Show, Sightings, Dead Famous, MSNBC Investigates, Jenny Jones, WB11, and numerous publications, including *The New York Times, New York Post, The Industry Standard*, and the *Philadelphia Inquirer*. She has been named "one of the 'top twenty' psychics" by Hans Holzer in *Woman's Own* magazine and interviewed on more than 150 radio stations, including one in Austria and England. Reuter's news media has featured her in Australia, Austria, Germany, England, Russia, and the major Spanish network, Telemundo. She has also co-hosted a psychic call-in show for eight years and has been featured in three books, as well as in *Woman's World Weekly* and *The Bridal Guide* magazine.

Jane also has the distinction of being retained as an expert government witness for a U.S. Postal Service investigation of a major mail fraud case involving psychic claims, assisted law authorities in cases of missing persons and homicides, as well as added to the history of New Jersey when her services were used for an archeological dig. For more than twelve years Jane was president of the Jersey Society of Parapsychology, founded more than thirty years ago for the purpose of providing mainstream scientific research and support to this field. Her ghost investigations have taken her to such notable places as the Lizzie Borden House in Massachusetts, the Palace Hotel in San Francisco, the William Heath Davis House in San Diego, as well as the Proprietary House in New Jersey, the only original royal governor's mansion still standing in the U.S. today.

Jane has graciously provided her psychic ability with my daughter's group New Jersey Ghost Organization– New Jersey Ghost Organization – on several major investigations and without her working closely, evaluating many of the artifacts that you will be reading about on the pages to follow, much of the information may still be buried in the realm of paranormal mist on the other side.

LISA PALANDRANO

At a very early age Lisa knew that her grandmother had died before anyone told her. She would get visits in her dreams from people before they passed over. This really all began when Lisa was twelve years old and it seemed that she always, as she put it, "knew things" and thought everyone had the ability to do the same. Lisa can see and hear spirits and "know things" at just about any time. When Lisa was around eighteen years old, she started sitting with groups of people who had the gift so I could strengthen hers. It worked and her ability increased tenfold.

Lisa has taken many metaphysical classes and will be offering classes of her own. She can work with many guides and angels, including the higher spirits such as Jesus and Mary. Between her many gifts she can also offer Shamanic Journey work and is a Reiki Master.

Lisa lives in Wanamassa, New Jersey, and is a valuable member of my daughter's group NJGO – New Jersey Ghost Organization and can always be counted on to produce positive spirit communication and information gleaned from residual haunting on investigations with the group. Lisa's help has provided information with certain of my artifacts in her evaluation of them.

MARYANNE VASNELIS

Maryanne recently became a member of New Jersey Ghost Organization and because of her ability as a psychic has become a valuable asset, not just to the group but also to myself in my working with artifacts.

Maryanne resides in Edison, New Jersey, and for as long a she can remember has had psychic feelings. Maryanne began taking classes in the 1970s in the hope of learn more that would help her to explain her feelings and the experiences that she had encountered during those early years. In attending the classes, Maryanne's psychic ability came to the surface to an even greater extent.

Having had many experiences with haunts, spirits, and ghosts, Maryanne continues to fine tune her psychic gift at every available opportunity and has participated on several investigations conducted by NJGO.

INTRODUCTION

I n 1954 I had the opportunity to become a Military Photographer by way of the proverbial "Greetings" that are all too familiar to those of you having been drafted into the service of their country. That which preceded and followed shaped my life and led me in the direction of seeking answers to what and who may still be connected to wartime artifacts.

My belief is that we are all born with a unique gift from our creator, a sixth sense, and the gift of "sensitivity." In some, this sensitivity may be at its highest level; in others it might be moderate or slight. Nevertheless, it is there and can be developed to various degrees. Throughout my life, I have experienced unusual and unexplainable feelings. These feelings were mild, but usually occurred when I handled certain artifacts, especially those having a wartime connection. Not having fully realized exactly what this meant, I became interested in exploring the paranormal and using the "Pendulum." My making a decision from the very beginning to never give direction to the Pendulum proved to be most significant in my being able to make the initial discovery of "Latent" energy, energy connected to artifacts.

Especially significant is the Pendulum that came to me at a crossroad in my life, shortly after my cardiac surgery. A religious organization, seeking contributions, had sent me a miniature wooden cross as a gift. Unique as it was to receive this cross, equally as unique was that I immediately made the connection to the wood cross that our Lord Jesus labored to carry on his last day on Earth. Now all that was left was to attach a piece of string and what took place from that humble beginning has been, and still is, a great experience, one that I will share with you in each chapter of this book.

By now, you must be wondering what all this has to do with "ghosts," "artifacts can talk" or "paranormal archeology" and I would too if I was not already aware and had not already experienced this paranormal nexus. In the following chapters, you will be enlightened, and somewhat surprised, at the truth that some "spirits," before continuing their journey to the other side, have chosen to stay behind because of an attachment to an artifact, providing information, giving us a better understanding of why and what we're dealing with, and how best to approach each situation. This experience or haunting may either be of the interactive or of the residual kind. Photographs of the artifacts presented here, and the investigation reports, will be presented in each chapter.

Can inanimate objects be haunted? Can spirits become attached to objects and cause unexplained events to occur around them? These and other questions will be answered throughout the chapters of my book. Latent energy, be it individual, collective or residual, can remain with objects after the passing of their owners because the owners have had a strong connection to these objects in life or because of their relationship to a traumatic event that had once taken place. Positive evidence obtained on an investigation can provide reasonable validation of a spirit presence. providing information that may not otherwise have been known.

At times, uneasy or unnerving feelings may be experienced when handling artifacts. Frequently, this experience occurs with items picked up on wartime battlefields, or artifacts that have remained in the possession of the original recipient until their passing, natural or otherwise. Most often, these conditions will produce positive indications that latent energy is present in the artifact. In my opinion, this is usually a strong indicator that a more extensive investigation may be warranted, one that may offer proof positive that a spirit is connected to the artifact. With possible identification of the spirit, disclosure and confirmation of specifics may lead one to reasonably conclude that the artifact is genuine.

History has provided the opportunity for paranormal events associated to persons, places, and things, and can best be defined as beyond the range of scientifically known and recognizable phenomena. Ghost investigators acknowledge that skeptics accuse them of seeing what they want to, or expect to, see. However, turn the argument around and say that the skeptics refuse to accept the possibility of what they cannot see!

Exploring the "Latent" energy experienced from inanimate artifacts, is a study of how energy remains with or around a specific object after the passing of an individual who had an affinity to it in life, or residual energy from an incredibly evil act left behind in its surroundings. After having been brought to my attention, many of the artifacts have revealed new, and sometimes startling, information, adding to that which might have already been known.

Since my days as a youth, during the chaotic wartime years of the early 1940s, my interest in the history of this period and the artifacts emanating from it has prevailed throughout my adult life. I must admit that in those early days, the word "paranormal" was unknown to me. My sensitivity would not flourish for many years, not until moving into a rental home in the New Jersey Shore area. With mail arriving for the first time, one envelope drew my attention. The return address indicated that it was from a religious organization; it contained a tiny, blessed wooden cross.

The evening before, I had been watching a television program in which experiments were being conducted with the use of "Pendulums." I decided to make one out of the wooden cross by attaching a length of string to it. My first experiment was holding the Pendulum over a photograph of my daughter and son-in-law with my dad, who would cross over several years afterward, standing between them. No movement was evident holding it over my daughter and son-in-law's head, but the surprise came when I held it over my dad; it began to rotate vigorously in a clockwise direction. Keep in mind, I had not given it any verbal directions; it was simply moving due to some unseen force. I decided to take this discovery a bit further and perform the same experiment by holding it over each of my classmate's graduation photographs in my high school yearbook. I recorded which of them it rotated over and those that it did not. At our 50th class reunion, discovering that those classmates who had passed on were the same whose heads the pendulum had previously rotated over didn't really come as a complete surprise to me.

My sensitivity, using the Pendulum, made me curious as to just what the reaction would be when applied to inanimate objects, not realizing the door that I was opening. This experiment would prove to become a source of valuable information. One of the most flamboyant, yet darkest, periods in history took place between 1923 and 1945 in Germany. The main contributing Axis nations, the Third Reich, Imperial Japan, and Italy, singly and together espoused intimidation, hate, torture, and murder. In part, these acts of fear and violence helped form the infrastructure of paranormal events, in combination with the many deaths associated with them. These traumatic energies, which arose from the ashes of the Second World War, will be remembered for generations.

In the many theaters of operation (Europe, Pacific, Asia, and North Africa), many Allied and Axis lives, including military, civilian, and those representing various government agencies, were lost during the battles; however, many lives lost were also lost to acts of torture and murder of civilians and prisoners of war. The disruption of lives during those turbulent times and the untimely loss of lives were contributing factors leading to paranormal events.

Of particular interest is the "Latent" energy left behind, the nexus to the badges, rings, uniforms, photographs, other artifacts from individuals, and from the battlefields, and other venues of this period. Many of these items were lost during battle and are still being recovered today. Referred to by collectors as Battlefield Pickups, War Booty or Spoils of War, they form only a small percentage of objects recovered among the lost items, most of which may never be found. Some artifacts are still in the possession of GI's who returned home, their surviving families, in private collections, and in museums. Other objects are still embedded in the earth, hidden by overgrowth or buried where soldiers fell serving their countries. New construction excavation sites have uncovered many such specimens, while others were obtained from men and women liberated from POW camps, civilians, and some from partially destroyed homes and other buildings. The energy from long past events, and the individuals who still linger, should be considered and recorded. This energy represents an eyewitness to history that still surrounds us, waiting to be acknowledged.

PART I

PARANORMAL ARCHEOLOGY

CHAPTER 1

A DOCUMENTED STUDY IN PARANORMAL ARCHEOLOGY

When first hearing or reading the words "Paranormal Archeology," the first thing that might come to one's mind is visiting battlefields with a metal detector and a shovel, however, a more accurate interpretation would be Military Archeology or Battlefield Archeology. There is a definite connection of the latter two to what I do. However, the main difference between military or battlefield archaeology and what I do is that I replace recovering artifact directly from the battlefield with recovering them directly from veterans who brought them back to their homes or estates or I recover these artifacts indirectly through those who do perform battlefield excavations. I also replace standard artifact analysis with the analysis of psychic intervention and interpretation. The correlation of my initial findings of what is known about the artifact, it's historical background, and what may not have been known is psychic intervention.

Little did WWII General Douglas MacArthur realize when he made his famous analogy that "Old Soldiers Never Die, They Just Fade Away" that this would, beside their memories, years later become a sort of paranormal epitaph. Their spirits may still have a strong nexus to their wartime places, events, and objects.

Startling paranormal insights emerging from the ashes of war torn battlefields of the Second World War, in Europe and in the South Pacific. They were also recovered from the home front and beyond. All were recovered from spirits still connected to their artifacts. This has opened the door to both discovering

16

new and important information and confirming that which may have already been known. By my presenting psychic and archive documentation, photographic and psychic evaluation of artifacts may be considered as proof that GI's returned with more than just memories and souvenirs. In some cases, the combination of evidence has been overwhelming.

Do you really know what came back in dad's duffle bag? After all, fighting on foreign soil, away from home, family, and loved ones must be worth something? Enter the spoils of war, war booty that quickly became a part of every GI's duffel bag. Recognizing every GI's desire to bring home some souvenir from the war, some of the firms in war ravaged countries that produced military badges and decorations continued to produce them for sale to civilians. These civilians in turn hawked these supposedly "authentic" war relics to soldiers on the streets, in beer halls, and in other dark corners following the war. Many GI's responded and unfortunately for them ended up snapping up newly minted war booty just as fast as the factories could produce it.

Most battle-weary GI's entertained thoughts of bringing something home from the war, other than a war bride, to be able to spin a tale for the folks back home of how he obtained the item. However, somehow, in many cases, the story did not exactly portray the way that the piece was actually obtained.

What does all this have to do with the paranormal? The GI's returning with genuine artifacts, especially those items liberated from individuals or battle sites, are the ones I and other paranormal archeologists are most interested in. These hold the key to unlocking the past through interactive spirits still connected with the objects or through residual projection or haunting.

Living beings function at a Bioelectric Cycle of 60 Hz. This enables our heart, brain, and central nervous system to function and communicate. Two-thirds of life exists with our mind and spirit. The other third is physical. Medically, the first law of thermodynamics states that energy cannot be created or destroyed, only transformed. So what happens to this energy when we die? Individuals who have passed on are capable of continuing to fully exist in the next dimension. They can communicate and interact with us. Spirits absorb surrounding energy, enabling them to not only communicate but to also make their presence known in other ways – through touch, by moving objects, and manifestation.

Everything around you is made up of energy. I look for "paranormal" energy using scientific equipment, along with the support of psychics' impressions.

There are two spirit types, interactive spirits and those in a residual occurrence, both of which are considered a haunting. An interactive spirit is just that. It is the soul of an individual who has passed on and continues to be observed in a location or locations. This spirit type can stay earthbound for a number of reasons. Typically, unfinished business will keep it earthbound – for example, the spirit needs to deliver a message, whether to just say I'm OK or I love you, or perhaps to provide a warning. At times they may do things to capture your attention, move objects, manufacture smells, attempt to manifest (like when you see a shadow or hear voices), and make noises.

A haunting defined as being residual is similar to a video playback. For my purpose, in researching artifacts, the scenario or traumatic wartime event that had once taken place is being played back and may be of significant historic value. In a residual haunting, the event, as it unfolds in front of you, provides you with no interaction between yourself and the images – the ghosts – that seem not to notice you as they go through the motions of an event that had once occurred. Residual is a left over latent energy or energy that is regenerated under certain unexplained atmospheric conditions which can be as simple as energy from an event recorded onto certain materials. Take something as average as a rusty nail in the wall or an old light fixture, both have the capability of recording all types of repetitious routines or activities.

How is this recording accomplished? In a similar manner to electronic and video recording equipment using audio recorders or videotape material. The older cassette, reel-to-reel audiotape materials, and most videotape are composed of about forty percent oxidized metal particles, more commonly known as "rust." This oxidized metal enables images and sounds to adhere to the surface; in the same way oxidized metals record sound and images on tape, rust records psychic sight and sound on ordinary objects. In the paranormal aspect, this process results in a residual projection or audio recording of a act or conversation that had once taken place during a different time period. More commonly referred to as a haunting, these recordings enable us to see past events as they had once taken place.

For a moment let us think in terms of a battlefield. The single most common experience that most people have reported has been residual sightings on or near battlefields. It is simply a playback of a recorded event that had once taken place in that specific location. When the conditions are right, you can see or hear this recurrence. According to science, everything is made of energy in one form or another. Looking at energy from the paranormal perspective, certain energy from an event can be recorded on various materials and played back when the atmosphere or conditions trigger it.

I consider a residual haunting that is connected to a wartime artifact, or any artifact for that matter, to be a time capsule. This glimpse back in time reveals a scene that, in retrospect, is historical and one that may not be discovered in any written wartime history. This type of haunting, when viewed, may seem a bit frightening at times, but you are in no danger.

A more common type of haunting in the investigation of artifacts is what is termed interactive. This is one in which a spirit makes its presence known in different ways. Most frequently a spirit connected to an artifact is seen in the psychic's vision as one attempting to communicate, sometimes quite vigorously. Interactive communication may reveal previously known information about an artifact confirming certain facts. However, equally important is information that had not previously been known. When this new information is researched, more often than not, it proves to be factual. I have found that when contact is made, the communication can move quite rapidly as some spirits have, in our time, waited for a long, long time to be able to make a connection. I have always been a willing listener and you should be too, but be sincere and ask the right questions.

The average individual may have fleeting glances of shadow images out of the corner of his or her eye or may have an unexplained feeling when entering a room or physically hear a sound or word, and, in part, this is what some mistakenly refer to as having psychic ability. Not so. These experiences are normal in some people. Having premonitions is a bit more in the psychic sphere and as you develop your sixth sense, which I believe we all have, your psychic senses will improve. My suggestion is that you read Psychic Jane Doherty's book, *Awakening the Mystic Gift*, if you wish to pursue this line of investigation for yourself.

In an interactive haunting you may encounter odors, voices, music, footsteps, a feeling of coldness, room lights may flicker or other strange noise may arise. Visible in photographs you may see a myriad of anomalies, varying from energy orbs, a slight touching sensation, mists, and strange lights to possibly a spirit image. This type of ghost may be the spirit of a deceased individual who, for varying reasons, is earthbound. This may be simply because the individual has not yet realized that he/she has passed on as the result of a tragic or sudden death, or it may be the result of a fear of moving on, some sort of guilt, or having left this realm with unfinished business. A spirit may also be here visiting loved ones, to warn or pass along a message for someone, or simply to join in the holiday festivities they have missed once being a part of. In passing, these spirits are the same as they were in life, both good and bad, and are looking for attention. They attempt to gain your interest by moving objects, making noises, touching, or in just about any way that they can.

These human spirits account for a majority of what I encounter when investigating wartime artifacts. I have devoted an entire chapter to the steps that I take when investigating an artifact once I discover latent energy is connected to it. Each step is carefully orchestrated so as to gain the most information, producing and providing to the paranormal community what I believe to be positive confirmation, proof positive that "Old Soldiers Never Die," or at least their spirits do not!

In the area of militaria collecting a question most often asked among both collectors and dealers, after the fact, is if the item that I just purchased is authentic? It seems that this is a common situation at most militaria shows throughout the country and, as a matter of fact, the world. Many were the times when I have seen collectors and dealers a scurrying helter-skelter, looking for an answer to this proverbial question. What if I told you that detecting latent energy connected to an artifact may be an initial step in determining the authenticity of an artifact and you were a collector or dealer. Would you believe me? Well, I can tell you that a considerable number have and have been thankful for it.

Now, what connection would detection of latent energy have with an artifact being authentic? This initial determination opens the way for the next step, psychic intervention. When it is determined that an interactive spirit is still with the artifact and is willing to communicate, the psychic can now begin to ask specific questions. Often these questions will bring answers as to the spirit's identity, why they are still with the artifact, etc.

Remember what I said earlier, you already possess knowledge of what the artifact is (in this case a medal) and you may have a story connected to it. Still, you would like confirmation of this, if for no other reason than to at least temporarily put your mind at ease. I say temporarily because there are additional steps to a thorough investigation involving an artifact.

Obviously, there normally will not be a psychic present at a militaria show, so what are your options? Earlier I discussed being able to receive an indication of latent energy from certain artifacts; this may be sufficient for some to conclude that the artifact is of authentic origin. This has been proven to be true many times through my investigation of artifacts. Actually, the successful use of a pendulum in this initial step has been ninety nine and nine tenths percent accurate.

Usually a genuine artifact has a monetary collector's value. How this value is determined is not important for this writing. What is important is that when an artifact is determined to have a spirit connected to it, especially if it should be a family member, it becomes priceless!

CHAPTER 2

USING THE PENDULUM AND YOUR SIXTH SENSE

What I do is a variation in the use of psychometrics. This is a form of extra-sensory perception in which a psychic is said to be able to obtain information about an individual through paranormal means by making physical contact with an object that belonged to that person. As I stated earlier, I am not psychic or clairvoyant; however, using the pendulum is where I feel that my sixth sense plays a part in the connection between myself, the artifact, and the spirit energy that surrounds it.

I have been asked many times why I don't use a pair of divining rods in my work? If I were to excavate battlefields, divining rods might help to locate the remains of soldiers, provided that the spirit energy was still there. Then again, all you may find is water. Divining rods (dowsing) are excellent in determining the extent of the auric field of a human being.

We all have a sixth sense with varying degrees of sensitivity, you simply have to develop and fine-tune it. If you are a parent, have you ever experienced thoughts, at times even fear, that your child may be in trouble or that something is about to happen? I know that I have. My mentioning earlier that as a youth, more often than not, I had experienced strange feelings when holding or being around the souvenirs that had been given to me by the neighborhood GI's returning from the Second World War. I had only come to the realization in my later years that this sensitivity was in some way connected to the paranormal, and began to fine-tune it through the use of a pendulum.

Author and pendulum showing how it is used to detect latent energy in the initial examination of an artifact. *(Photo Credit – Author's Photo)*

I hope that what I'm about to tell you will be a new experience for you, one that will help to open the door to the past. If you have or have inherited military artifacts or are a militaria collector, you have what may become the experience of a lifetime awaiting you. You can do it!

When first attempting to use the pendulum as an instrument to detect latent energy, my suggestion is to not give any directions to it, simply let the pendulum do its own thing, whether it is to be in a rotation or a swinging motion, or to remaining motionless. The pendulum will remain motionless when no latent energy is detected or, in the case of photographs, when persons have not yet passed on. I will explain this a bit more as we go on.

I'm certain that most of you already are aware of saying a prayer prior to beginning an investigation and an additional prayer before leaving the location being investigated. If you do not, I recommend that you consider doing this, if for nothing more than your own peace of mind. An opening prayer that is most used is one to Saint Michael the Archangel.

"Saint Michael the Archangel, defend us in battle, be our protection against the malice and snares of the devil. May God rebuke him we humbly pray; and do thou, O Prince of the Heavenly Host, by the power of God, thrust into hell Satan and all evil spirits who wander through the world for the ruin of souls. Amen."

When working with my artifacts I have adopted using the Prayer to St. Michael before I begin any investigation. At the conclusion, I use a slightly modified closing prayer.

"In the name of Jesus Christ I command all human spirits to be bound to the confines of this artifact. I command all non human spirits to go where Jesus Christ tells you to go, for it is he who commands you, Amen." When I evoke the closing prayer at a location I substitute the word artifact with the word location. Even if you are not a very religious individual, I suggest that you try using prayers, beginning and ending. I have never experienced any residual aftereffects from an artifact, but it can't hurt and you may feel a bit more at ease.

One other item that I feel should be brought to your attention early on is that when using psychic intervention, as I do, that the information received must be sorted out and applied to what may already be known about the artifact. You may find that, at times, bits and pieces of what you feel may be unrelated information may actually be remotely related. This you will discover during your after research. Adding to what I have just said, there may also surface some information that is not related, along with the possibility of an unrelated spirit popping in.

When investigating an artifact at home, it is best to do it in seclusion and under quiet conditions; however, this is not always possible when on location at a museum or a private home. Working with an artifact can be done at any time of day or night, enabling you to detect any latent energy, should it be present. There are other possibilities for detection of a spirit presence at the same time, once you have detected latent energy connected to the artifact.

It is important to note that you should work with only one artifact at a time, with no other artifacts in close proximity, to avoid an overlapping of energy fields and not being able to accurately detect which of the artifacts the energy is connected to.

Only recently have I added another phase when investigating an artifact, speaking to the spirit who is present, and receiving answers through my pendulum. You can relate this to a similar reaction found when using a Ouija board. Should you attempt this, I recommend that you use a voice recorder to record the session. A spirit will interact with you if you open yourself up to that spirit and treat it like it has a mind and intelligence. In other words treat spirits as you would any human in this earthly realm, with respect and dignity. Ask questions where responses can only be yes or no, asking the spirit to move the pendulum in different directions for yes or no responses. My preference is asking for a rotation when a yes answer is required and to swing for a no answer. There may be times when the pendulum will vibrate slightly; this usually happens when the spirit is hesitating on an answer. This may be for various reasons. The spirit may not know the answer or may be confused due to several thoughts being asked in the one question. For best results you should always keep your questions simple, yet carefully formulated to give you the information that you're seeking, e.g. are you willing to speak to me? Questions require multiple thoughts from the spirit are not the best to ask, e.g., are you a male or female? Asking the latter type of question is when you will receive a hesitation from the spirit. Keep in mind that your sensitivity may only be with the use of the pendulum and not with clairvoyant, clairaudient or other psychic abilities.

For this phase you can use either analog or digital voice recording devices. I will usually set up both types of recorders when working at home. On location, I will usually only use the digital type. When using either type, I recommend the addition of an external microphone for best results. On some voice recorders you may pick up internal noise when relying on just the built in microphone. Remember, you are not directing you questions to the artifact itself, but to the spirit presence with the artifact.

There are two techniques that you can use. Before beginning any recording, it is always a good practice to state your name date and time, and the time when ending it. When sitting with the artifact you can hold the microphone while recording or if you decide to not ask questions you can leave the recorder sitting near the artifact and leave the room for a period of time, keeping it on the record setting. Before leaving the room, always ask the spirit that if the spirit should wish to say anything, that the device on the table will record the words or message. If the spirit wishes to speak, it will. Spirits will embed their voices on either the tape of the recording device or other media that you may be using at the time. It's not like you or I speaking out verbally. At times a voice recording will be very clear and may at other times be muffled, almost indistinguishable as being human. When playing the recording back, you must listen carefully and I recommend the use of a headset for this purpose.

This same thought process should be considered when, and if, you decide to enter the next phase of your investigation, voice recording or EVP (Electronic Voice Phenomenon). EVP captured with voice recorders using tape is usually considered to be more acceptable by the scientific community than EVP recorded on digital recorders, mainly because one has the physical tape in hand. Remember the Golden Rule, speak unto others as you would have others speak unto you!

Before I decided to attempt using my pendulum as a tool to answer yes or no questions, fostering communication with the spirit attached to an artifact, I first experimented with this on an investigation with my daughters paranormal group, New Jersey Ghost Organization, on one of their major investigation of a haunted theater. Reporters from two local newspapers were present that evening and some startling results were captured on digital camera, video, and on our voice recorders.

The following is the results of my test that evening. Here is the transcript of my simple questions and the spirit presence's responses. Psychic Lisa Palandrano, present that evening, previously confirmed parts of this conversation with us, along with physical experiences of some of the theater members. It also shows that you may receive conflicting responses, something that must be accepted when engaging in this phase.

CIRCLE PLAYERS THEATER

JULY 29, 2007
OLYMPUS VN960PC VOICE RECORDER
Q & A DIALOG
LOCATION: DRESSING ROOM - 6:26 PM

If any spirits are present, the instrument that I'm holding is a pendulum. It will not harm you and you may use it to communicate with me by responding to my questions with a yes or no reply.

If your reply is no please make the pendulum swing back and forth.

If your reply is yes please swing the pendulum in a circular motion.

Is there anyone here who wishes to communicate with me this evening? You're indicating No.

Are you afraid to speak with me? You're indicating No again.

Haunted Circle Players Theater in Piscataway, New Jersey.
(*Photo Credit – Karen E. Timper, NJGO*)

Is there any reason that you wish not to communicate with me tonight? You're not giving me an answer.

Are you afraid of me? Yes.

You don't have to be afraid of me, I'm not going to hurt you. I want to find out who you are, possibly why you are here, and are you friendly.

Are you friendly? You're indicating Yes.

Is there anyone else here with you tonight? You're not answering me again.

If you don't mind, let me ask you one more question ... Can you see me? Yes.

Are you a man? Yes.

Are you a woman? No.

Are you part of the theater group? You're indicating a no response.

Were you here when this building was a school? You seem to hesitate.

Were you here when this building was a grange? You're hesitating again.

Are you more than 50 years old? You're giving me a yes answer but you seem to hesitate a little.

Are you still afraid to speak with me? Yes.

Are you more than 50 years old? Yes (Repeat question but more positive response).

Are you more than 100 years old? You're telling me yes but do you mean that you were here more than 100 years ago? Yes.

Did you belong to an Indian Tribe? Yes.

Is there anyone else here with you this evening? Yes.

Do you realize that you have passed on? Yes.

Are you trying to communicate with people here? Yes.

Do you pull people's hair? Yes.

Do you do this often? Yes.

Do you push people? No.

Do you make sounds or make noises? Yes.

Are you happy here? Yes.

Do you wish to leave here? No.

(Strange noise noted at 9.25 on my voice recorder).

Did you die at this location? Yes.

Was there an accident? No.

Were you killed here? No.

Did you die of natural causes? No.

Was there anyone responsible for your death? You're hesitating. Whoever this is seems confused.

You indicated that you're an American Indian or an Indian. Is that true? Yes.

Was there a battle of some sort here? No.

You indicated that the person with you is a male. Is that true? You started to say yes, then went to no. You seem to be confused again.

Do you know where you are? You say no but now you seem confused again.

Why are you so confused? Is it because you don't know what happened to you? You're hesitating; you're going back and forth.

Does this other individual with you wish to speak with me? No.

Are you in need of any help? Yes, with a hesitation.

Is there a way that we can help you? Yes.

You said that you want to stay here. Is that true? Yes.

You're happy here. Is that true? Yes.

You just want to remain here and harm no one. Is that correct? Once again you are hesitating.

I'm going to take that as a yes.

Can you see me? Again a weak hesitation.

Can you make your presence known in another way? No.

Hopefully well be able to talk again later - Thank you.

END DRESSING ROOM 7:05 PM

The subject of EVP is discussed in detail in Part III.

PART II

ARTIFACTS CAN TALK

B efore beginning this section, there is some information that all readers should know about the format used in this section. At the beginning of each chapter I will present a brief history of the artifact. This pre-known information is never given to any of the psychics beforehand. I will at times introduce questions or make statements that are relative to their findings and under certain circumstances will reveal bits of information during the session. This is done to help trigger deeper psychic impressions or to respond to one of their questions to me.

As most psychics are aware, but some readers may not be, psychic sessions may be brief at times and lengthy at others. Once the "psychic door" has been opened, some spirits associated with the artifacts may come through immediately and may leave shortly into a session. Other spirits that may not be directly connected to the artifact, that are with the spirit, may come through to help. In some situations, psychic impressions may have been received directly from the artifact itself and not the spirit.

Clearly, the psychic impressions session in each chapter strictly records the psychics' impressions. What I have stated at the beginning of each chapter cannot influence the psychics. It is important for me to emphasize that the psychics are never privy to this information.

CHAPTER 3

THE LEGACY

Of particular interest is the legacy that Adolf Hitler and Reichsführer der SS Heinrich Himmler left for future generations, one surrounded in mystique and evil, embedded as a part of history forever. Beginning as Adolf Hitler's personal bodyguard, the SS soon transformed into one of the Third Reich's most infamous organizations, steeped in the occult, pagan rituals, and Celtic symbols, this ritualistic brotherhood was shrouded with secrecy. Heinrich Himmler created his own version of Camelot, securing and restoring a seventeenth century castle in 1934. The castle was located in the Village of Wewelsburg, 15 km south of Paderborn in Westphalia. Sitting atop a limestone rock overlooking the Alm Valley, this magnificent three-century-old structure was rented from the District of Buren for the symbolic fee of only one Reichsmark per annum. In the closing days of World War Two, the castle was partially destroyed on March 31, 1945, by the direct order of Himmler. All that remained standing were the outer walls.

Himmler designed a unique skull ring for his SS organization, with Celtic symbols. Each ring has the engraved names of "H. Himmler" and that of the recipient, along with a date on the inner surface. Many individuals have experienced unusual feelings of evil or despair when possessing one of these rings. This feeling is not surprising when one considers the circumstances surrounding the rings. When the recipient of a ring was either killed, or passed on naturally, the ring was to be returned to Himmler, and placed in a resting place of honor at Wewelsburg Castle.

It has been alleged that when U.S. troops came upon the castle, the officer in charge discovered a box containing a large quantity of the rings and distributing them among his men as souvenirs. Should this have been the actual memorial case, where are the rings today? After the war, a thirty-year reconstruction of the castle began in 1949 and was completed in 1979. The castle is open to the public as a museum, housing many of the symbolic trappings from its former SS occupation.

THE HALLOWED HALLS

In 1948-49, the castle was restored. The castle was then reopened as a museum and youth hostel, while adjacent to the castle, the Niederhagen camp kitchen had been renovated into a village fire station. To the surprise of some who have visited Wewelsburg Castle, a feeling of coldness and of evil has been experienced when walking the corridors, as if the spirit of Heinrich Himmler himself is walking beside them. Visitors have felt cold wisps of air, the smell of a burning candle, and the glimpse of a hasty shadow out of the corner of an eye. Was this wishful thinking or simply an overactive imagination? Possibly it was H.H. himself or one of his "Twelve Teutonic Knights" paying their respects? On moonlit nights the castle presents itself as an eerie silhouette against the open sky. The lower chambers of the castle's north tower, the most sinister of all, were where ritual ceremonies were preformed. The circular construction of the crypt added to its ritualistic atmosphere and surrounding the walls were twelve pedestals, each designed to house the urns of cremated ashes for each of Himmler's Twelve Teutonic Knights, should they meet their final demise. This was to be their final resting place, including the man himself, Himmler!

SS TOTENKOPF HONOR RING
1933-1945

The following information was excerpted with the kind permission of Don Boyle from the revised edition, third printing of his book, *SS Totenkopf H. Himmler Honor Ring 1933-1945*. Don's first edition was published in 1993. A second edition was published in 1994 and his third edition in 1995. Lauded among militaria collectors, Don is considered a foremost expert in the field of militaria, and is more affectionately known among his friends and throughout the militaria-collecting community as the "Honor Ring Man." All editions of his book are presently out-of-print.

The first appearance of the Honor Ring was in 1933. SS-

The infamous SS Totenkopf Honor Ring. (*Photo Credit – Author's Photo*)

Chief Heinrich Himmler gave it as a gift to high-ranking officers of the Army and SS. One such officer was General Hans Lammers, Chief of the Reich Chancellery from 1933 to 1945. He was issued an SS-Honor Ring for his participation in "The Night of the Long Knives" when Adolf Hitler purged his own army on June 30, 1934. Lammer's ring is engraved with that date and was personally presented to him by Himmler. Himmler also promoted General Hans Lammers to honorary SS-General in 1940.

On 13 September 1936, the SS-Totenkopf H. Himmler Honor Ring was instituted by Heinrich Himmler as one of the highest ranking SS awards and accompanied with a certificate. The rings were awarded for personal achievement, loyalty, and duty to Adolf Hitler's ideologies.

Most SS-Honor Rings were awarded on 20 April, which was Adolf Hitler's birthday; however, many were also awarded on specific holidays and events related to the rise of Nazi Germany. The rings were only to be worn on the ring finger of the left hand.

Since the SS-Honor Ring was of special significance, both the ring and certificate could be taken away from any SS-Officer who resigned, retired, was suspended, demoted or discharged from duty. Rings and award certificates could be reinstated to the officer if he were accepted back into the organization. Any officer who died had his ring returned to the SS-Personnel Office for preservation and storage.

By the order of Reichsführer-der SS Heinrich Himmler on 30 October 1944, further formal presentation of the Totenkopf Honor Ring were cancelled; however, some were still issued privately until April 1945 to qualifying SS officers by Heinrich Himmler.

The pagan runic symbols on the honor ring come from the German mythology found in Germanic, Danish, Norwegian, and Swedish beliefs in Nordic supremacy.

All SS-Totenkopf Honor Rings were made of silver. In German mythology, the God Thor possessed a pure silver ring on which his people could take an oath of loyalty. The Totenkopf Honor

Rings were die cast then hand tooled and highly polished. The top of the ring had a smiling skull with crossed bones on each side of the skull; separated by oak leaves was a sigrune in a triangle, separated by more oak leaves is a swastika in a diamond, more oak leaves, then a circle with dual sigrunes and a tyr-rune, then more oak leaves and a hexagon with an asterisk in it. All these were Nordic ritual symbols. At one time the swastika was the highest form of good luck one person could have. Many turn-of-the-twentieth-century buildings still have the swastika on the floor tiles and ceilings.

The inside of all rings is engraved with the initials "S.lb." that stands for *Seinem lieben*; translated it means with respect and honor, the last name of the recipient, date of presentation, and the name H. Himmler.

Initial investigation of the ring, using a pendulum, evoked an extremely strong reaction of latent energy surrounding it. Very little information, other than what may have been obvious, was known about this ring.

PSYCHIC IMPRESSIONS: (ANONYMOUS)

"I'm receiving a feeling of water; that the individual was under water, cool ocean water. I'm visioning a man in a plane wearing an oxygen mask and flames. The name of 'Hodge' came through expressing something about exemplary achievement and firepower. A second impression was that this ring was found in dirt, the sight of a man about 45 years of age with dark hair wearing a beige barrett and short pants with suspenders.

Was he the individual who had found the ring or who had owned it? Is there blood on the hands of the person who had worn this ring? We may know more in the future but until then, you must be the judge."

PSYCHIC IMPRESSIONS: PSYCHIC JANE DOHERTY

Our session began, as most of our sessions do, by Jane relaxing and placing herself in her psychic mode. I had let Jane know that this was considered a ring of honor and of loyalty.

Jane slowly picked up the ring and held it cautiously between her two fingers and as she began to visually examine the ring her facial expression suddenly changed from curiosity to surprise before she blurted, "Oh! There is a symbol of a skull on the top of it. That's odd to me."

I asked Jane to take special notice the symbols on the edge, that they are Celtic symbols and to look inside the ring. There is a name etched inside the band, but only one name. Usually there are two names. The only name engraved in this ring is the name H.Himmler, which means the individual's name must have been removed.

"Richard, I still cannot overcome my shock that the image of a skull could represent honor and loyalty. The shape of the skull has had various meanings throughout the world. As you can see, I have crystal skulls and they are with me when I do psychic readings. It would be interesting to know other meanings for the skull shape and its connection to Hitler and the Third Reich. Let me see what psychic impressions I receive and then we can talk more about the skull shape."

"You reacted strongly to the skull shape. Do you have any psychic impressions why Hitler, Himmler, and others used the skull shape?"

"The shape of the skull has had several symbolic meanings throughout the centuries and in different cultures. The skull represented 'man conquering death' to the Christians. The image has been depicted on women's pins, so the wearer could ward off evil. The Mayans revered the image and believed it represented a higher power. The pirates adopted it and used the image for their flag, but added cross bones. Today, the skull is used on bottles of substances that could be poisonous. There are also crystal skulls today who some believe have magical powers or hold information that could benefit humanity. Hitler probably used it because he thought it was a talisman that would bring him the 'power' to win. He thought it protected the wearer much like a religious icon. Those who believed in his ideals and were worthy enough were honored with an award that included this symbol. Wearing this symbol assured him that he had God's Power with him at all times."

Closing her eyes, she tightly grasped the ring for a few seconds in silence before she excitedly said, "The energy emanating from the ring is remarkably strong. It is much stronger than the other ring I held. Wow! The energy is penetrating through the other side of my hand. It's beginning to feel hot to touch. I don't feel the person who owned this ring died in the war. The ring is holding too much latent energy for it to belong to someone who may have worn it only during the war before he died. The heat from the ring makes me feel it is branding an image of it into the palm of my hand. That is just too much energy. The person who owned the ring died at a much older age and several years after the war. Now, do you know if the soldier died in the war or not? No, you see, when the war began to near its end things began to fold rather quickly and confusion set in. Therefore, some soldiers could have simply kept the rings."

Staring into the corner of the room with her eyes unfocused, Jane suddenly said, "I am receiving another impression. I can see a vision of a soldier standing over the body of a comrade. I can see him bend down and retrieve something in his hand. I interpret this image to mean the soldier took the honor ring off his comrade's finger. However, instead of returning it, he removed the name of the soldier and kept it for himself."

CHAPTER 4

THE HINDENBURG
LZ-129 HAUNTING

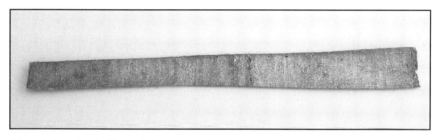

Singed three-inch sliver of the outer skin of the Hindenburg LZ-129 has a residual haunting connected to that horrible day in 1936. (*Photo Credit – Author's Photo*)

As fate would have it, a gentleman, with several of his friends, from Columbus, New Jersey, made an eleventh hour decision to travel to Lakehurst, New Jersey, to be on hand for the scheduled arrival of the Giant Airship LZ129 Hindenburg at 7:25 P.M. that evening, May 6, 1937. Barely arriving on time, seeing the giant airship already visible in the stormy sky over Lakehurst, the men rushed to where most of the spectators gathered. Working their way through the crowd, chaos began as the night sky turned red. People began running from the tremendous flash of the explosion. The Hindenburg was being consumed in flame. The aluminum structure was beginning to crumble under the tremendous heat being generated as the giant of the sky crashed to the ground.

During the ensuing ciaos, tiny pieces of the "skin" (outer covering) of the airship fluttered to the ground, one piece landing near where the gentleman from Columbus was standing. The piece was still aflame. He immediately stepped on it to extinguish the fast-burning flame, as he wanted it as a remembrance of the scene he had just witnessed.

Close-up showing a part of the singed area. (*Photo Credit – Author's Photo*)

Arriving back home, he thought it a good idea to cut the postcard-sized piece into slivers, one for himself and a piece for each of his friends. One of the skin slivers now resides in my archives.

PSYCI IIC IMPRESSIONS: PSYCHIC LISA PALANDRANO

Holding the tiny piece of outer skin in her cupped hands, Psychic Lisa Palandrano's first reaction was startling.

"My hands felt hot, very hot! A woman's face briefly flashed before me and I can hear sounds of screaming, of running, and a great deal of terror. I see the letters HIN and I'm being directed to the top right portion where a fire that is engulfing what appears to be a flying ship began. This is where this piece originated."

Not known previously to me was the location on the giant airship from which the piece had originated. Since this evaluation I have made several visits to Lakehurst and its infamous haunted Hanger No.1.

Extremely haunted is the tarmac area in front of the famous Hanger No.1 and inside the hanger at the NAS (Naval Air Station) at Lakehurst, New Jersey. Voices have been heard revealing the mass confusion related to the disaster of that infamous evening, May

Haunted hanger No.1 at Lakehurst Navel Air Station, Lakehurst, New Jersey, exhibiting the WWI camouflage paint pattern on the 1,500-foot structure. The two-leaf sliding, counterbalanced doors at each end of the hangar are massive; each door leaf weighs 1,350 tons and measures 136 feet in width, 177 feet in height, and seventy-six feet deep at the base. (*Photo Credit – Karen E. Timper, NJGO*)

6,1937, when thirty-six unsuspecting individuals, returning from an air voyage to Germany, lost their lives in a ball of flame in a matter of only a few seconds. From inside the hanger, at times when no one should be present, the whirring of engines can be heard. At times a lone, misty figure has been seen lingering high on one of the overhead catwalks, near the roofline, and when called to, there is no reply. On some evenings, near one of the night security lights inside the hanger, what appears to be a figure can be seen, when security personnel move toward it for a closer look, the figure seems to vanish.

When I had the opportunity to discuss this with Psychic Jane Doherty, I was informed that when she had the opportunity to visit this area many years before visitors were actually permitted to, at the request of base personnel, that a small building to the right of the crash site, when viewing it from the tarmac in front of Hanger No.1 was used for the actual temporary morgue. Some of the bodies were immediately transported to area hospitals.

Thirty-six people had perished in this horrific accident so it is not surprising that spirits still haunt the tarmac and the hanger that once housed this magnificent giant of the sky.

CHAPTER 5

HAUNTED PADLOCK OPENS DOOR TO WWII DEATH CAMP'S PAST

Haunted padlock and key from Dachau concentration camp, rusting and time worn, reveals its past use. (*Photo Credit – Author's Photo*)

GUARD DOGS AT DACHAU

When first becoming aware of this padlock's existence and not being told anything other than it was a lock and key, I anxiously awaited the photographs that were being emailed. Upon opening the attachments, not knowing what to expect, having high hopes that I would detect latent energy with my pendulum, I was not in the least disappointed.

Holding my pendulum in front of the first image, it immediately began to rotate vigorously, the reaction I had hoped for. There was no need to examine the remaining photographs, as the strong reaction that I had received was sufficient to warrant additional investigation.

Keep in mind that details may vary slightly between psychic impressions and is frequently the case. However, when you consider what they are experiencing, when relating them to known details, they are in fact very similar. Using two psychics provided a confirmation of known information and the opportunity to uncover a wider span of previously unknown information.

IMPRESSIONS FROM TWO DIFFERENT PSYCHICS

First Psychic (anonymous) provided the following evaluation, "Ouch, did this one give me a jolt! Prison, I get prison, and old prison. I definitely see a high wall and the smell of horses; this lock has been somewhere near stables. I'm also getting the smell of fire, like a campfire. I see a wooden door and hear someone saying – get in the hole – and then the lock clicking. I'm getting the word old being repeated over and over. This lock was used in many different time frames. Someone said it lasted. When and wherever this was, it was always in places where there was suffering and conflicts. A voice is telling me that this was brought over; giving me the impression that they're telling me that the lock came to America on a ship."

When I informed the owner of the lock what the first psychic's evaluation was he quickly responded. "I don't know what to say! According to the veteran who brought this padlock back from WWII it came from a concentration camp his unit helped to liberate; that it was used to lock up the guard dogs; your psychic was nearly right on the money! The smell of horses could easily have been the smell of dogs and they used wood burning stoves for heat in the camp buildings; again your psychic was also right about the lock returning aboard a ship."

After a few weeks had passed, the lock's owner contacted me to inform me that he decided that he wanted to rid himself of the lock. He was offering to sell it to me if I was interested. I subsequently did purchase it for my archive.

PSYCHIC IMPRESSIONS: PSYCHIC JANE DOHERTY

Before Jane reached for the lock to hold it she scrutinized it for several seconds. She hesitated at first to touch the artifact, which made me anxious to know why. So, I questioned her by asking if she was afraid to hold it? Her response was quick in coming. "No. I am just trying to release the eerie feeling I sense when I look at the lock."

I next asked Jane if she felt bad energy around it? Her response was quick. "Yes, there is an unusual energy coming from it, but I do not know yet if it is bad or what it means."

I handed Jane the lock. She closed her eyes and grimaced as she held the lock in her hands. I waited anxiously for her psychic impressions to emerge.

After a brief hands-on session with her eyes closed, Jane confidently stated, "There is an extreme amount of energy still held within the metal of this lock. As I tighten my grip around it, I feel as if the lock is pulsating small ripples of vibrations. The energy is heavy and pervasive and probably laden with a lot of emotions. In fact, I am beginning to feel an overwhelming sadness and a queasy feeling in the pit of my stomach. I need to stop for a moment, so I can gain control of my emotions."

I never realized how personally affected a psychic could become receiving impressions. I asked Jane if she felt that she would be able to continue the session? "Yes, I just need to take a moment to release the emotions, so I can concentrate on trying to see images or hear sounds." Jane closed her eyes again and waited for more impressions to come forth.

"I see an image of someone incarcerated and I hear voices shouting and screaming. I see prisoners and sense death. This lock is somehow associated with death. Oh! I see the name Nazi spelled out in my mind's eye. The lock is from WW II. This lock must have been used in a German concentration camp to lock up prisoners or associated with a concentration camp or the area near one. Now I know why I have had such a sick feeling holding this lock! It is associated with death. Wait! I am hearing the word 'gold'. Could gold be associated with the lock? Were some locks made of gold?" I responded that I do not recall that any would have been made of gold but that perhaps gold has a symbolic meaning.

After several seconds in silence again Jane revealed more. "This is horrific! The Nazi's associated the death of a prisoner to 'gold'. It was an honor and a show of loyalty to Hitler to carry out an execution of a prisoner. The murder of a prisoner had a symbolic value equivalent to gold. This is disheartening. I do not want to receive any more impressions from this artifact!"

After Jane's session with the lock, I again contacted the former owner to apprise him of Jane's evaluation. His response was immediate. "Very impressive! I seldom pay much attention to the sometimes quite elaborate stories veterans tell about their items and experiences. I considered that if his story was true, the use of your services could prove most interesting, and it has! Actually, I'm amazed! This has been an eye opener for me and I have enjoyed the experience … thank you." M.W.

Additional note: The German manufacturer of this lock is still in existence and has confirmed that it was produced by their company and the time period, bearing their nostalgic logo "ABS."

CHAPTER 6

A FOOTPRINT IN TIME

THE HAUNTED SOLE

During an excavation on the Belgium-Luxembourg border, a unique footprint in time was uncovered from a WWII battle site. Just below the ground's surface, a deteriorating sole from the boot of a German soldier slowly became visible. Unique may not be the word to use for this find; eerie may be more appropriate. A long lost sole of a tortured soul.

The haunting is believed to be residual, since the information received was not obtained from the sole of the boot directly. Small amounts of rust particles from the metal heel plate and earth residue from the sole were all that was used for evaluation by the psychic. It was not possible for the psychic to know where this rust/residue material originated or the object it was from.

For those who may not be familiar with the term "residual haunting" it is used to describe the energy of a past situation or event having been captured and recorded. This recording is simply being played over and over similar to a looped video. The spirits involved are not interactive, meaning that you cannot converse with them or they you.

A frequent occurrence in paranormal investigation is a residual haunting. As I had mentioned earlier that oxidized metal, rust, is a common recording element for a residual haunting as it reacts similar to that of coatings that were used on older video recording tapes. The participants in a residual haunting are more commonly referred to as true ghosts!

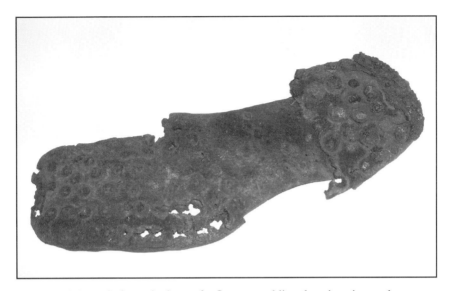

Battlefield dug sole from the boot of a German soldier, deteriorating and very haunted. (*Photo Credit – Author's Photo*)

PSYCHIC IMPRESSION (ANONYMOUS)

At first when the rust particles and sole residue were held by the psychic, words began to emerge: "Patriot, Belgium, bullets, machine gun fire, and co-patriot." Next, some startling information began to present itself. "There is a strong connection to a soldier having some connection to a camp, possibly nearby in Belgium. Mounds of dirt, death, and shoes walked on those individuals buried beneath the mound. I see a man with a rounded helmet, soldiers sitting around saying there is no God; they laugh at this, then one silently cries. This camp ended by being blown up and the soldiers were actually happy to be captured, they wanted it all to be over. One soldier received burns on one side of his face, blisters, hot, his face melting; he screams out to the God that just a few minutes ago he denied existed."

PSYCHIC IMPRESSIONS: PSYCHIC JANE DOHERTY

When I asked for a second psychic evaluation from psychic Jane Doherty, strong feelings began to emerge in Jane.

Assertively, Jane revealed, "There is blood mixed in the dirt on the bottom of this sole. When I focus on the remnants of this boot sole, I see a pool of blood seeping from the sides of it. Then I get a vision of dead bodies strewn across a battlefield and someone walking in the area where the dead bodies have fallen. Now, if you or I saw blood on the ground, we wouldn't intentionally walk through it; we would try to avoid it. However, the soldier who wore this boot had no aversion to the Death he witnessed. He walked right through the pools of blood near the bodies. Now, I see an image of what I feel is a German soldier kicking the bodies of the dead enemy soldiers, probably to try to verify their deaths."

I asked Jane if she was receiving any names? Her response to my question was, "yes, I hear the name Herman. It could be a first or last name. I sense his personality is authoritative and arrogant, which gives me the impression that he is an officer."

When sessions such as this ends, one always has a feeling of sadness; one which quickly turns to a lighter feeling, knowing that those who had passed on are now in a better place.

CHAPTER 7

D-DAY HAUNTING

THE NECKLACE

A hand-carved wooden symbol liberated during one, if not the, most bloody and significant invasions in world history took place on June 6, 1944, D-Day on the beachheads of France. The significance of the letter "D" in D-Day was used in short for the word Disembarkment.

Ste Mere-Eglise stood in a pivotal location between Cherbourg and Caen, whose capture fell to the U.S. Eighty Second Airborne Division. Unfortunately, sections of two planeloads of parachutists (parachute infantry divisions were divided into sections) from the Second and Third Battalions of the Five Hundred and Fifth Parachute Infantry were dropped directly over the village.

To make the decent even worse, a farmhouse had caught fire either from tracers or the preceding aerial bombardment and illuminating the entire surrounding sky, making perfect targets of the descending paratroopers. Many were killed on their way down and at least two were drawn into the fire itself. The loss of many more lives came from some paratroopers being entangled in trees and on roofs, becoming easy targets for the German troops on the ground.

After the initial excitement of battle was over, the German troops went back to their beds, under the belief that the immediate threat was over. Unbeknownst to the Germans, Lt. Colonel Ed Krause, commander of the Third Battalion of the Five Hundred and Fifth had landed just one mile west of the village and quickly began gathering stray men. Within an hour he had managed to round up approximately one hundred and eighty men and began heading straight into the village.

This hand carved walnut symbol taken from a German soldier on D-Day has a story to tell. (*Photo Credit – Author's Photo*)

Since the German garrison had gone back to bed after all the initial paratroopers had either been killed or captured, Lt. Colonel Krause, not aware of this, was able to enter the town unhindered and was shown the German billets by a local Frenchman whom they ran across. Thirty Germans were captured and about ten more were killed, while others fled into the nearby wooded areas surrounding the town. By six a.m. Lt. Colonel Krause had secured the village, cutting off German communications and the main route between Cherbourg and the remainder of the German Army.

One must take note that this French town of Ste Mere-Eglise was where, following this parachute assault, the famous statue of a paratrooper hanging from a church steeple has made it's mark in history and has been reenacted in the motion picture *The Longest Day*.

EARLY IMPRESSIONS BY PSYCHIC LISA PALANDRANO

The necklace was liberated from a German POW taken at Ste Mere-Eglise by Sergeant "Ace" Ferbie of the Third Battalion, Five Hundred and Fifth Infantry of the Eighty Second Airborne Division on June 6, 1944. Ace crossed over in 1996 at the age of ninety ... R.I.P.

PSYCHIC IMPRESSIONS: PSYCHIC JANE DOHERTY

Jane's first comments had a tone of sarcasm as she stated, "So, this is a real swastika on a gold chain that someone actually wore as a piece of jewelry. I have seen this symbol in pictures, but I never thought I would actually ever hold one!"

I began by asking Jane if she would be able to receive impressions even though she seemed repulsed by it? Her immediate response was positive. "Yes. I just have to focus on being objective and not allow my personal opinion of the symbols cloud my psychic impressions. Fortunately, I did not live through that era, so my emotional connection is limited to what I learned in history class. So, it should not be too hard to receive impressions and interpret them objectively."

Jane closed her eyes to concentrate on the necklace. She seemed to shift the necklace from her right hand to her left hand as if she tried to feel which hand assisted her best in stimulating psychic impressions in her mind.

Several seconds in silence prompted some quick impressions from Jane. "I am getting an auditory impression. I hear the name Carl and a word that sounds like Gustof. Gustof could be the name of a person or the name of a town or area associated with the necklace in some way. I do not know how this piece of jewelry was actually used during WW II, but I sense this particular artifact was used as some sort of 'lucky charm'. The soldier who wore this swastika believed it had a protective quality. I can see some sort of ritualistic movement used around this artifact."

Jane, I need to tell you what I know about this type of jewelry. German soldiers often made items while waiting in the trenches before the enemy advanced close enough for action. It is possible this type of item was made to send home to a wife or girlfriend. However, the swastika symbol was used in all kinds of ceremonies and rituals. So, that may be the connection you are making to the necklace. What you seem to be identifying is how the symbol may have been used, but it may not pertain to this particular piece. I just wanted to give you that information so that it may help clarify your psychic impressions.

Jane responded quickly, "I feel this necklace served as a personal talisman. The German soldier probably made more than one necklace. He kept one for himself and sent the other to his girlfriend. The necklaces were matching pieces so the couple believed the energy connected to both would keep them emotionally connected and the 'love' and the 'soldier' safe during the war. However, I do not think the soldier lived long enough to go home."

"No matter how many rituals the German soldier used to infuse into the necklace, it didn't bring him much luck!"

CHAPTER 8

COFFINS OF STEEL

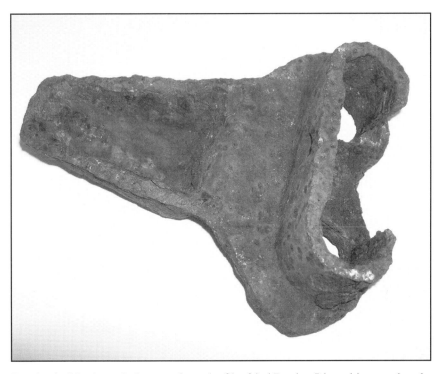

Dug in the Northern Ardennes along the Siegfried Bunker Line, this rusted tank track coupling has both a residual and interactive haunting attached to it. *(Photo Credit – Author's Photo)*

GHOSTS OF BATTLE

Unearthed during the Battle of the Bulge in the Northern Ardennes, somewhere along the infamous Siegfried Bunker Line, was a rusty, triangular-shaped piece of iron that was once a part of a U.S. Sherman tank. Identified as a track coupling, this and many other pieces lay strewn about, some partially buried under the earth's surface. Only chunks of armor plate, along with other remnants, were left as grim reminders of what had taken place over fifty years prior when this tank exploded. This tank track coupling was from a tank unit that was part of the United States One Hundred and Sixth Infantry Division, a division that had received the brunt of the German Ardennes Offensive. The One Hundred and Sixth was forced to retreat and in a few days, just over the Belgium border, surrendered the greater part of their division to the Germans. The spirits connected to this artifact appear to be an unusual combination of residual and interactive.

EARLY IMPRESSIONS BY PSYCHIC LISA PALANDRANO

"I see a convoy or row of trucks and other vehicles traveling on dirt, no grass but many trees. There are many what appear to be soldiers but a bit confusing as some are wearing a greenish-gray uniform, while others are in some sort of khaki uniforms. I'm picking up excited words, some in English and others in a foreign tongue. Three individuals seem to be connected to the vehicle this piece came from that has been literally blown to pieces. They keep flashing before my eyes. They seem to be crowding and pushing each other as if they want to communicate."

PSYCHIC IMPRESSIONS: PSYCHIC JANE DOHERTY

Jane reached for the piece of metal and held it between her two hands before she stated, "The vibrations from this piece of metal are very strong. When I close my eyes, I see an army vehicle. It is the lead tank in a formation of other moving tanks. I get the name Peter, but I am not receiving any other impressions about the name. However, I can't seem to release the name from my mind. It just mentally repeats itself every few minutes. Now, I can see tanks moving towards a hill and then the image seems to disappear. When I concentrate this time, the tanks disappear from view. I believe the 'lead tank' blew-up! This piece of metal is from a destroyed tank."

I then revealed to Jane the fact that this type of American tank was prone to easy destruction because of thin armor plating. They were fast, but flimsy and easily destructible. You are holding a piece of iron that is part of a Sherman tank that had been blown-up and completely destroyed. Chunks of armor plating were strewn all over the area where it was excavated.

"I sense that this tank was hit, while the operator tried to give instructions to the other tanks. This battle either ended quickly or the other tanks retreated after this lead tank was destroyed."

CHAPTER 9

GHOSTS OF THE MASK

CRIES OF A LONELY SOLDIER

L ocated several years ago by a WWII veteran that somehow was drawn back to the now serene islands, where he had once fought in one of the largest blood baths of the WWII Pacific Campaign known as Bloody Nose Ridge on the Island of Peleliu (Beliliou). While scuba diving near Bloody Nose Ridge, a large coral ridge line that overlooked what was once a WWII Japanese airfield on the island, he became curious as to what he might find if he explored the cave that he had noticed half way up the cliff that was overlooking the lagoon. Deciding to make the climb, thoughts began to flash through his head as he recalled events of the invasion he participated in over fifty years ago on September 15, 1944. Upon reaching the cave, entering cautiously, he moved forward slowly as the cave was lit by the minimal amount of sunlight entering from the tiny opening in front. If it was not for his foot accidentally hitting an object on the cave floor he would never have made the discovery of a rotting remnant of a gasmask that had remained untouched for these many years. This artifact is itself unique as wartime Japanese artifacts are scarce. Most of these artifacts deteriorated rather rapidly due to the damp jungle conditions, more commonly known as jungle-rot.

The Japanese garrison on Peleliu under the command of Lt. Gen. Sadao Inoue was 10,500 strong prior to the U.S. invasion. After seventy-four days of fierce battle, the island was considered secure by U.S. forces. The Japanese forces had all but been

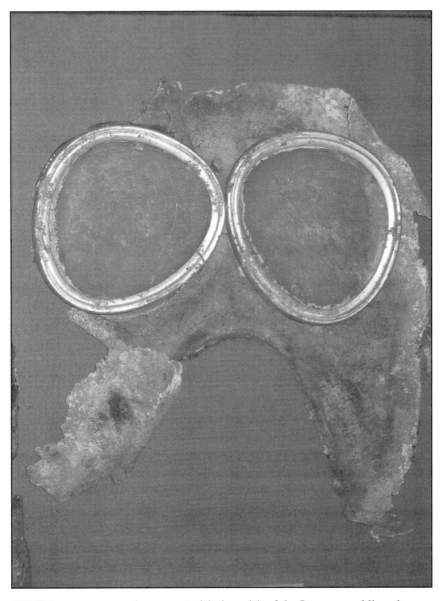

WWII Japanese gasmask remnant with the spirit of the Japanese soldier who died wearing it, along with three unknown ghosts, still haunting it.
(Photo Credit – Author's Photo)

annihilated with only three hundred and twenty prisoners surviving; one thousand one hundred and eighty Japanese had died honorably for their Emperor.

EARLY IMPRESSIONS BY PSYCHIC LISA PALANDRANO

During this brief psychic evaluation, a strong feeling emerged that someone had been killed wearing this mask. What Psychic Lisa Palandrano encountered was the interactive spirit of a Japanese soldier who spoke freely. "I would like to see me son again, to go back home to my family." This is a situation where the individual had not yet realized he had been killed. I had received this artifact from the grandson of the veteran and was informed that the evening before shipping it to me, when he was retiring for the night, he experienced many flying beetles invading his bed. They seemed to swarm out of nowhere. Could this vision of bees have had some connection to the soldier to whom the mask belonged or could it have been an indication of what was to come or may yet come to be experienced with this artifact? If you look closely, perhaps you will see the face of the helmeted Japanese soldier wearing this mask.

PSYCHIC IMPRESSIONS: PSYCHIC JANE DOHERTY

Jane quickly stated, "This mask makes me shudder. There is a powerful energy field around it. When I hold the mask, the energy goes right through me. It is a cold, damp-like feeling that gives me 'goose bumps'. I am not yet sure, but I think a 'spirit' is attached to it. I sense death around it, but more than just the death of the person who owned the mask. Every time I hold the mask, it seems like my personality tries to change.

I have to control myself because I want to shout and yell out commands. I also get feelings of anger and extreme agitation, but these are not my emotions. That is why I think an entity is attached to the artifact."

I asked Jane if she felt that the spirit is confused or maybe evil?

"I cannot tell, yet! The person who wore this mask was strong-willed and ruthless. This time when I try to 'tune' into the latent energy, I hear sounds that have a choppy cadence to them. I am not familiar with the language. It doesn't sound like a German accent. It sounds gibberish. I can also see that the terrain is different. It looks tropical, so it must be associated with water. Can you give me some details about the war? Sometimes, details and questions can stimulate or be a catalyst for more psychic impressions."

I revealed the following information about the artifact to Jane: this was from one of the bloodiest battles the Marines had in the South Pacific, which was on the Island of Palau, at Bloody Nose Ridge. The mask was taken out of a cave many years after the war and this was the island where women were jumping off the cliffs with their babies, the ones that had gotten together with Japanese soldiers. The Japanese were really defeated, I forget how many thousands of men. There was only a handful that had survived the battle; the whole garrison was there and this was a Japanese gas mask. In case there was a gas attack, they would put this on to be able to breath so as not to be overcome by the poison gases.

"This is a Japanese gas mask? I don't think he died from gas, even though this was a protective device. I can see that several soldiers, including the one still wearing this mask, were killed in an attack. There is gun fire and explosions coming in all directions."

What I would like to find out is who this individual was connected to this mask, to get a name, a unit number, and if he's trying to communicate.

"I certainly feel death around this, as though something is still hanging around it. I would look at this as an artifact that is haunted. I definitely would feel that with it. Interesting, because I do get an image of a man, how I describe the man, he's short, a lot of the Japanese are short but I could see an image of a man that's short and I'm getting a letter 'A' but that is all."

What I picked up I thought was the discoloration of the lenses and one of them I see an image of what appears to be a Japanese soldier. You can see the Japanese hats that they wore had a flap on them, looks like a flap coming down the sides. It appears that the gas mask is on in the face that I see.

"Faces and things, that's a very individual thing and as a psychic it's not where I go. People have sent pictures that they see a spirit in but I don't see it. If I were to see anything, I see more ghost faces so I'm seeing, yes, I see three to four ghost faces in here where I'm looking. It almost looks like the faces I have in my stone. Now, you will see up here there are two eyes, a nose and a mouth, there's another one next to it. Ok, do you see that, and there's another one next to him and I go here, that's where I first got something, there something over here but those two are very clear to me. So, I don't see what you see but see there are faces."

"It would be difficult to communicate with the spirit by just holding the mask. There may not be enough energy to connect with him. Yes, I certainly feel death around the mask. I do feel that it is haunted, but I would not want to try to communicate directly with the spirit attached to it. There is a negative energy field surrounding it. You really should take some measures to protect yourself. You need to cover it in sea salt for a week or so to help dissipate any negative energy still emanating from it. The energy feels disruptive and could stimulate 'fights' in people who absorb its energy!"

Jane concluded the session by stating that, "I can unequivocally state that this mask is HAUNTED!"

CHAPTER 10

A HAUNTING NEXUS TO A WWII GENERAL

UNITED STATES BRIGADIER GENERAL BEVERLY C. DUNN

CAMERA WITH A PARANORMAL NEXUS

This camera was the property of United States Brigadier General Beverly C. Dunn and was used from the beginning of the Second World War until the end.

Brigadier General Dunn served as District Engineer at Seattle, Washington, in July 1940 and in March 1942, and was assigned to the North Atlantic Engineer Division in New York. He became Deputy Chief Engineer at Headquarters SHAEF in February 1944. Shortly before the dissolution of SHAEF, he succeeded General Hughes as Chief Engineer.

My preliminary pendulum examination of the camera indicated a high latent energy level. Since this camera is of the older cassette-to-cassette 35mm type, the film had to be loaded by the user into one of the cassettes, then attached to the spool in the receiving cassette, so when taking photographs it could be advanced from one to the other. Since there was no provision for

Having been carried all through WWII, this general's camera imparts its unusual story. (*Photo Credit – Author's Photo*)

rewinding the film, it had to be advanced to the receiving cassette completely before removal for processing.

PSYCHIC IMPRESSIONS: PSYCHIC JANE DOHERTY

Jane began the session by saying, "While I hold the camera, I hear the word 'Dutch' and I see a photo of a windmill and a ship. I do not feel strong latent energy coming off the camera. There is energy, but it feels dispersed. I believe the owner of this camera took a lot of pictures of Holland. Did the Americans go to Holland?" Yes. "Because I am picking up Dutch. There were definitely pictures taken in Holland. I definitely feel there were pictures of Holland."

I interjected the possibility that this person could have traveled to the Netherlands because he was in Europe.

As the evaluation continued Jane stated, "A lot of pictures were developed and sent home before the war ended. Some of those pictures were published in a local newspaper, magazine or some other type of publication. If you can get the film still in the camera developed, the photos would be featured in a publication. The photos did not get developed, because the soldier lost the camera towards the end of the war."

What is unique about this camera is that it's the older type that used two film cartridges. In one of the cartridges fresh film, cut from a bulk roll, was loaded and as you advanced the film it moved completely from one cartridge to the other. This film had to then be processed, usually by the people themselves or by a processing facility. This camera still has film that had been exposed in the receiving cartridge.

In ending the session Jane stated, "Oh, you got to get that developed because I'm probably seeing something in the future that pictures from that are going to be published."

The film from this camera is in excellent condition considering the length of time that it has been in the cartridge. It can be processed. Hopefully, I will be able to locate a professional lab that specializes in black and white processing, as none of the current one hour processing services are equipped to handle it.

CHAPTER 11

I.D. BRACELET
WITH A PAST

Sterling silver identification bracelet that is named on the front, with the serial number on the reverse, exhibits considerable wear to the surface finish, along with some damage. (*Photo Credit – Author's Photo*)

Very little was previously known of this WWII identification bracelet other than, by the name engraved on the front, that it had belonged to a Lt. Van Zutphen L.A. A stamping on the reverse indicated that it was produced by the firm of Kreisler USA in .025 gold on sterling. When examined by the psychic, startling information began to present itself from the interactive spirit connected to the artifact.

PSYCHIC IMPRESSIONS: PSYCHIC JANE DOHERTY

After concentrating for a moment Jane stated, "When I hold this ID Bracelet, I get a distinct feeling the soldier who owned it was an officer. I can see a map of the United States, and I am looking towards the west, but not the West Coast. I sense it to be more in the middle of the map, so the soldier who owned this is probably from the Midwest. I do feel that he died in the war and this was something sent home with the remains."

You can see that it's bent a little bit out of shape.

"Yes, I can see that but I do not know how or why it is bent. I believe the soldier's mother kept the bracelet and wore it at times to honor the memory of her son. Then it was displayed along side his picture in the family home. Near the end of his parents' lives, I feel they moved, and the bracelet was thrown in a box and probably lost in the move. I hear the word Lieutenant. Are there lieutenants in all branches of the service or just in the army?" Yes, there are lieutenants in all branches of the armed services.

Jane continued, "I see an image of a ship, so I can interpret that image to mean he was an officer in the navy. I also see an image of New Orleans. Perhaps, he visited there before he left port. Where are the naval ports in the United States?"

Some of the ports were in Norfolk, Virginia; New York; San Diego, California; Groton, Connecticut; and possibly one or two others here in America.

"I do not get the impression he was stationed in San Diego. I get a more connected feeling to Norfolk, Virginia. I also see an image of a submarine. He may have been a commander or officer in the Navy and was on a submarine or always wanted to be on one."

CHAPTER 12

HAUNTING HORROR OF WAR

When I first received an email from a fellow militaria enthusiast telling me that he had been receiving very bad vibes when handling this WWII Japanese Type Fourteen Nambu pistol, along with certain other wartime artifacts in his collection, my interest was piqued. I told him to send me, via email, a picture of the pistol. Immediately, using my pendulum, I received a very strong indication of latent energy being present. I had been told absolutely nothing of the origin of the pistol and, when I forwarded the picture to one of the psychics who evaluate artifacts for me, as I usually do, I did not tell her anything about the pistol, other than what was obvious. Her reply was almost immediate.

PSYCHIC IMPRESSIONS: PSYCHIC LISA PALANDRANO

"I get the sense of extreme fear, guilt, and abuse. It seems the last owner of this gun used it in threats and execution style killings. The fear from the victims is still there and I feel the person doing the killing had a lot of guilt, even though he didn't show it. If someone wants to keep it and not harbor those feelings, it needs to be cleansed with some white sage while invoking the white light."

Japanese WWII pistol tells of a deadly but remorseful spirit's past involvement. (*Photo Credit – F.H.*)

Death March

Is it possible that this pistol may have been carried and used by a Japanese officer on the infamous Bataan death march that took place in the Philippine Islands during the Pacific campaign in the Second World War? Through extended investigation we may some day know.

The infamous Bataan Death March: (also known as The Death March of Bataan) took place in the Philippines in 1942 and was later accounted as a Japanese war crime. Logistics planning to move the prisoners of war from Marivele to Camp O'Donnell, a prison camp in the province of Tarlac, was a sixty-mile march that occurred after the three-month Battle of Bataan, being part of the Philippines (1941–42) during World War II.

The march, involving the forcible transfer of tens of thousands of prisoners of war, moved the surrendered remnants of the combined United States personnel and the Philippines home defense forces from the Bataan peninsula to prison camps. This march was characterized by wide-ranging physical abuse, murder, savagery, and resulted in very high fatalities inflicted upon the prisoners and civilians along the route by the armed forces of the Empire of Japan. Beheadings, cut throats, and casual shootings were the more common and merciful actions, in comparison to the bayonet stabbings, rapes, gutting incidents, numerous rifle butt beatings, and a deliberate refusal to allow the prisoners food or water while keeping them continually marching for nearly a week in tropical heat.

Prisoners were attacked for assisting someone falling due to weakness, or for no apparent reason. Strings of Japanese trucks were known to drive over anyone who fell. Riders in vehicles would casually stick out a rifle bayonet and cut a string of throats in the lines of men marching along side the road. Accounts of being forcibly marched for days with no food and a single sip of water are in postwar archives, including filmed reports. The exact death count has been impossible to determined. (Wikipedia encyclopedia)

Here is the response from the current owner of the pistol: "Richard, thank you so much! I have to say this has been a real help to validate what I have felt so strongly."

PSYCHIC IMPRESSIONS: PSYCHIC JANE DOHERTY

Jane hesitated to take the pistol from my hand. Once again, the expression on her face showed fear.

"As I hold this pistol, I feel 'cold' and I am 'trembling'. The owner of this gun killed just as many innocent people as he did soldiers. It seemed to be a sport to him. I see a lot of brush and tropical-like plants. I get an image of oriental-looking people who I sense are shorter than average height. They are probably Japanese. There are men in uniform, but I also see others who are not in uniform. I can see quick, darting moves. As I try to focus on the image, I can see a lot of people gathered on the sides. I think what I am seeing are prisoners. Could this be a battle somewhere in the Philippines?" Yes.

Continuing, Jane stated, "The owner of this pistol still has an angry, murderous spirit. I feel this pistol holds a lot of residual energy or a spirit is still hanging around it. I would cleanse this pistol good. Also, I feel it is better displayed than handled because of the negative energy surrounding the pistol."

On this note the session ended; however, I decided to ask Jane what her opinion was in the use of a pendulum, that I had a recorded session on video of an associate of mine using a pendulum to determine information about an artifact that may have a spirit still hanging around it.

Jane's response was quick and to the point, "A pendulum can read latent energy and can provide other information about an object if you phrase the question in a 'yes' or 'no' format. You do not have to be psychic to use one. The pendulum has been used in map dowsing to locate areas for various reasons. In fact, I used the pendulum as a tool to tune into my subconscious mind in order to bring intuitive information into my conscious awareness, when I first began developing my psychic ability. If you use a pendulum on this pistol and ask if it is haunted, you will probably get an affirmative answer."

JAPANESE NAMBU PISTOL

I wish to sincerely thank the owner of this pistol, who was kind enough to contribute the following information, based on his experiences using a pendulum. I'm honoring his request to keep his name anonymous; he is a long time collector of militaria who has just begun experimenting with the use of a pendulum on specific artifacts in his collection. The following is his story about this specific Japanese pistol.

My first encounter with this Japanese WWII Type 14 Nambu pistol was about seven years ago at a southern gun show. I was able to negotiate a cash/trade. I must say that in my initial assessment I felt a pronounced difference in this pistol from that of another which was included in the deal. This Nambu pistol not only possessed all the trademarks of a combat used pistol, it had its own emotional feel as well. I had mentioned to my wife later that I had a feeling of desperation as well as a general feeling that this weapon had possible seen too much during it's use and long life. This was one of the few weapons or military items that I ever felt so strongly about. Before sharing the rest of this truly bizarre ride, I must say that I'm not seeking any opportunity to convince anyone with the information that is about to unfold. I wish only to share this and let it stand as something to consider and for you to analyze further.

I guess it's best to start at the beginning; while surfing the Internet one day, looking and reading about all things related to military collectables, following this area like others follow the stock market, I chanced upon Richard's website and was very intrigued by what I read and saw. There have been many times where I have often considered that items owned by an individual or group can hold certain energies. However, I had never considered exploring any further, at least until now! Curiosity, to say the least, had gotten the better of me and of course that led to my using a three inch steel cross, a piece of string and much more than I bargained for. Looking back now in retrospect I went immediately to the Japanese Nambu as if that was the only place to start. Setting the pistol on a small wooden table, holding the pendulum over it, I watched in disbelief at how quickly the steel cross began to spin, as if it was motorized. Barely being able to hold onto the string, I became speechless as well as being, at the truest level, *freaked out*!

After taking a needed break for some fresh air and some reassurance that I had not lost my mind, I went back in to see if it would do it again. I am sure you know the outcome already and I went back to the computer to begin my quest, reading anything to do with the use of the pendulum, seeking anything to help me define what I have experienced. During this study, I discovered that some people engage the use of the pendulum for advice and meditation. I decided that I really had to take this one step further, to see if I can communicate with any entities that might be attached to the pistol.

Making the decision to be as safe as possible, I surrounded myself in God's light, saying a prayer of protection, and jumped in headfirst. My first thought was to establish with whom I may be in contact. I hoped I would be communicating with the owner of the pistol. My opening statement asked that they only speak if they are a child of God and wish no harm. Thankfully the reply came through with a positive answer. The spirit coming through was that of a male and I wish that I could describe the electricity of that initial exchange; I was starting to be aware of a very different feeling in the room, as well as the physical effect that this first encounter was starting to produce within me. I began to realize that I was getting impressions in my head almost as if I was starting to sense another person's presence, as well as their personality. Needing another break, trying not just to leave the house like a scared rabbit, I went outside for another breath of fresh air just to clear my thoughts about what had just happened.

At this point, my wife came in and I informed her of this entire strange scenario. Well, to make a long story short, she needed some fresh air and the same reassurance as I did a few hours earlier. The interesting thing is she now wanted to see if the male spirit would talk to her, but he seemed to want no part of any communication with her. We both had the strong sensation he may have been offended by her attempt to communicate. It appeared in later sessions that other women being present also offended him; he would not talk to them. I will elaborate on this further as we discover more about this man and get a real glimpse of his story, as well as the true man he is now in the spirit world.

CHAPTER 13

STEVE'S TREASURE

This artifact is one that is very dear to my heart that was given to me by my wife's brother Steve when we visited with him on a vacation in Long Beach, California, several years ago.

Steve was a career Navy man, retiring after thirty-two years of active service. Beginning just prior to the United States involvement in the Second World War, 1940/41, his ship was in port at the Suez Canal, North Africa. A British soldier walking sentry duty on the dock immediately below Steve's ship noticed Steve on deck near one of the ship's rails and called to him, "Hay Yank, can you spare some cigarettes, got a ring I'll swap ya for a few packs." Complying with his request, Steve now became the owner of what was to prove to be a very unusual skull ring. The "Tommy," as Steve put it, told him that he had liberated the ring from a German airman, after his aircraft had been shot down in a raid over Malta shortly before his being transferred to the Suez. Steve truly surprised me by making a gift of the ring, something that I did not expect. I was extremely excited about now having this tiny piece of history, completely blackened with years of oxidation.

Before continuing, I must tell you that on occasion Steve had worn the ring. After the war an unfortunate incident occurred. Steve was stationed in San Diego, California, and during the loading of a Navy truck, closing the tailgate, his hand became caught and the ring had to be cut from his finger.

Knowing that Steve would be interested in seeing the militaria collection of a highly respected collector living in Long Beach, we drove to this individual's home. With his

This solid silver ring was retrieved from a German WWII aircraft that went down in flames during the battle of Malta. (*Photo Credit – Author's Photo*)

help, I was able to determine that the ring was not of World War Two vintage, but rather of World War One origin. The ring depicted the skull symbol of the German Ninety Second Infantry Regiment - Brunswick. The big question now was, why a WWII German Airman happened to be wearing a ring from the First World War? In all probability, a family member of the Airman had served in the Ninety Second Infantry Regiment - Brunswick and had given him the ring to wear for good luck. It was also possible that the Airman served in this WWI regiment, as there were many older individuals serving in the Second World War, who had also seen service during the First World War. It was not uncommon to have this overlapping by individuals having service in two different wartime periods or branches of the military.

Upon our returning home from vacationing in California, I immediately took the ring to my jeweler to have it repaired. My second surprise came when he cleaned and polished it and informing me that the composition was that of solid silver. Now that the oxidation was gone, its original beauty was emerging.

Historical note: On 10 December 1940, the German OKW High Command issued a directive ordering the transfer of the German Tenth Fliegerkorps to Southern Italy and Sicily. Their first official action was off the Pantelleria against a British convoy on 10 January 1941. From the sixteenth to the nineteenth of January 1941, air strikes directed against Malta commenced. Records indicate that ten out of an approximate force of eighty aircraft had been confirmed as being shot down in the raids over Malta during this time period. A Stuka is a back-to-back two-man aircraft, with the pilot in front and a second crewman facing the rear as an aerial gunner.

EARLY IMPRESSIONS BY PSYCHIC LISA PALANDRANO

During the investigation session my psychic, being told absolutely nothing about the artifact, immediately began to receive impressions. While holding it in her hand she asked an intermediary by the name of Mary, to aid her, telling Mary that, "she saw a male who seemed to be present, but would not communicate with her." Mary began by stating that, "he did not wish to talk about the ring, but that she could provide some information. At one time this ring was in dirt and that the number 34 was important. This was either the year when he was given the ring or the age when he died. He had died wearing the ring."

PSYCHIC IMPRESSIONS: PSYCHIC JANE DOHERTY

As Jane held this ring, staring at it, she stated, "This is another ring with an image of a skull carved in it, but I do not feel repulsed by it like I did with the first skull ring (referring to the SS Totenkopf Honor Ring). I also feel this ring is older than the other one I held. Maybe it is not from the same time period. The latent energy is strong but does not feel negative. I think more than one man might have worn it, because the energy pulsates at different rates and in several directions."

Do you know anything about this ring?

"Yes, I keep seeing an airplane, so I feel the ring was worn by a pilot."

I told Jane that the ring dated back to a regiment in World War I and that there were many older men from that war who also served in WWII. It is possible that someone owned it in both wars and an individual in WWI later gave it to another member of his family.

"I do sense that the owner of this ring survived WWI, and that he gave it to his son as a good luck piece. The original owner believed the ring was blessed with protective powers and could bring his son back from the war safely, as it did him. Actually, I think the son survived the war."

CHAPTER 14

BLOOD OF TWO ENEMIES

I t is truly amazing what you can find on some Internet auctions. While scrolling through one such auction, I came across a Second World War Japanese type ninety-nine military aviation camera with the original red filter, wooden box case, and the official certificate dated to 1945. This official certificate, stamped and signed by an officer, gave the GI permission to either send or to personally bring it home. In this situation, the GI decided to send the camera home. However, psychic intervention seemed to indicate that the GI might not have made it back home himself.

As always, when holding my pendulum up to the photograph of the camera on my computer screen, the reaction was extremely vigorous, indicating a strong latent energy connected to it. At this point I must tell you that the photograph was of the camera in its wooden box case and the certificate was propped up on the inside of the open lid. Taking a closer look, the certificate seemed to have some sort of stain and at the time I had thought that it might have just been from moisture. However, the surprise was to come later!

The day had arrived when I received the shipment of the camera, and the fun began. I first had to have the Japanese writing that was on the labels to the wooden box case interpreted, so I contacted a collector who I had known for years who specialized in wartime Japanese items.

Examining the certificate closely, I became curious about the stain, due to the color. At first blush that stain had appeared to be from moisture; however, the brownish appearance, combined with the aging of the paper, raised the question, could this be blood?

Now this really piqued my investigative instincts and I had to find out if the stain was blood. Then the next question would be, whose? Fortunately, the name of the GI, his rank, and the official stamp of the A.P.O (army post office) with the unit number were

Many wartime photographs were captured with this Japanese aviation camera, but they pale in comparison to what unfolded with the certificate, the one giving him permission to send his captured artifact home.
(Photo Credit – Author's Photo)

on the certificate. These details can make research easier; however, that is not always the case.

I first began examining the certificate with the use of my ultraviolet light, but to no avail. I next decided to obtain a vial of luminol. Luminol is a versatile chemical that exhibits chemiluminescence, with a striking blue glow, when mixed with an appropriate oxidizing agent and is successfully used in crime detection of blood.

To exhibit its luminescence, the luminol must first be activated with an oxidant. Usually, a solution of hydrogen peroxide (H_2O_2) and a hydroxide salt in water is used as the activator. In the presence of a catalyst, such as an iron compound, the hydrogen peroxide is decomposed to form oxygen and water: $2\ H_2O_2 \rightarrow O_2 + 2\ H_2O$. In a laboratory setting, the catalyst used is often potassium ferricyanide. In the forensic detection of blood, the catalyst is the iron present in hemoglobin. Enzymes in a variety of biological systems may also catalyze the decomposition of hydrogen peroxide. When luminol reacts with the hydroxide salt, a dianion is formed. The oxygen produced from the hydrogen peroxide then reacts with the luminol dianion. The product of this reaction, an organic peroxide, is very unstable and immediately decomposes with the loss of nitrogen to produce aminophthalic acid with electrons in an excited state. As the excited state relaxes to the ground state, the excess energy is liberated as a photon, visible as blue light. (Wikipedia encyclopedia)

At the time of this writing, every attempt is being made to locate existing family members of the GI for additional information. The camera itself is now undergoing restoration to bring it back to working condition.

PSYCHIC IMPRESSIONS: PSYCHIC JANE DOHERTY

Jane briefly held the certificate and immediately began to speak. "There are two different blood stains on this certificate!"

This statement had caught me completely by surprise.

Jane immediately followed this by saying, "I am getting an unnerving feeling, very bad, from the one stain. This one belonged to the enemy. However, the other one is more calming and was made by the individual who carried this certificate. He had it in his possession when they both were killed. I have an image of a physical struggle between the two men and another image of others off in the distance. I can see a gun directed at the soldiers and both of them fall down. I think the bullets, fired unintentionally, may have been responsible for killing both of them."

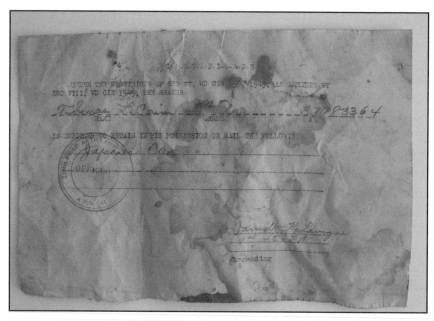

Close-up of the haunted, blood stained certificate. (*Photo Credit – Author's Photo*)

CHAPTER 15

A HAUNTING CONNECTION: ANNE FRANK

During the Second World War, Germany boasted a myriad of military awards, the silver oak leaves being one of the higher ones. Officers and men of all ranks within any branch of the Wehrmacht (military), Waffen-SS (the fighting branch of the SS) or the auxiliary service organizations who had previously been awarded the Knight's Cross were eligible to earn the silver oak leaves. The Knight's Cross with Oak Leaves was the next higher grade of the Knight's Cross above the original, and, as such, was an even more highly regarded award.

These silver oak leaves found their way into my possession quite unexpectedly. Before moving into my current home, while living in a home in the New Jersey shore area, one of my neighbors was moving and, knowing my interest in military artifacts, had asked if I would like to have these. He told me that he had brought this and a few other items back from WWII. Being that he was alone and had no family, he wanted someone else to have the items rather than having them go astray. I gladly received the gift and told him that I would never sell these artifacts.

Note, for the militaria enthusiast, on the reverse of this artifact is stamped the German silver content mark and the manufacturer's logo.

While I did not wish to keep you in suspense so long, I felt it important to present some background to this artifact, keeping the premise in mind that some who will be reading this book may have no knowledge of the background of military awards and decorations.

These silver oak leaves were one of Germany's higher awards to be added to the Knight's Cross or to the Iron Cross. This example has a passing connection to Anne Frank.
(*Photo Credit – Author's Photo*)

I could not wait to get home and to put my pendulum to this artifact. Immediately the pendulum began to rotate, giving me a stronger than usual reaction. I felt that this tiny piece of history held a story just waiting to be told. Since my daughter's paranormal group had a scheduled meeting that evening, I decided to bring it with me and have one of the psychics give me a hand in its reading. The unexpected happened!

PSYCHIC IMPRESSION (ANONYMOUS)

Contact had been made with a woman and the following information came forth with high emotion, "This is connected to an office in Belgium, a woman, and WWII. This woman was somehow connected to Anne Frank's family. I don't know how, but when I hold this, I see the vision of Anne's face floating in front of me! She (the woman) was the lover and fled with her boyfriend, not her married lover. She (the woman) was sorry and didn't want to die. The name Rosalie or Rosalia is coming through. May God forgive her, there was nothing she could do."

The woman's married lover was quite possibly a German officer at the office in Belgium."

PSYCHIC IMPRESSIONS: PSYCHIC JANE DOHERTY

This was one of the few times that I felt that Jane should have some basic historical information about an item. This was an award, an addition to one of Germany's highest awards, and would be attached to the Knight's Cross of the Iron Cross. The only award that was higher than these oak leaves included crossed swords added to the oak leaves.

Jane began by stating, "So, it was a very high award for this person. Would 'Engo' be a German name? I don't know what are many German names. So, just take note of that name, 'Engo'. I feel this belonged to an officer. This was given to him as some type of award after he won a battle. I am not familiar with battle names, so you would have to give me some names to focus on. I would then be able to sense what energy around the battle name gives me a more connected feeling."

There were so many that it would be difficult for me to begin to name them, I replied.

"Let me concentrate to see if I can get any bits of psychic impressions that could be a clue to the identity of the battle. Okay. Now I hear voices speaking what I believe to be French. I am almost certain it is French because I studied that language in high school. I see an image of a map. I seem to be focused on a border area, which I sense is probably the battle name. If I had to guess, I would say it is the Alsace-Lorraine region of France."

The Germans advanced quite rapidly through that region before they occupied most of France.

Jane continued, "What it feels like to me, it's like an early accolade of things, not towards the end but early is what I am feeling."

CHAPTER 16

THE SILVER TRAY

This silver tray, originating in Germany, found its way to me by way of Argentina and was once the proud possession of a family with the last name of Buderer. What is not known is if the Bruderer family immigrated to Argentina or if this tray was sent to another family member when the Bruderers passed on. The Bruderer family had a son by the name of Hans who had served in the Abwehr during the Second World War. The Abwehr was a German intelligence organization, existing from 1921 to 1944.

Because of the dimensions, my belief is that it was used as a calling card tray. It has the following inscription on the obverse, "Von der Frontkamaraden d.I. Abt. 10/IR. 45" (From Comrades at the Front).

Close-up of the presentation inscription on the front side of the tray.
(*Photo Credit – Author's Photo*)

This tiny silver tray is worn and has a clandestine connection to Hitler's Germany. (*Photo Credit – Author's Photo*)

PSYCHIC IMPRESSIONS: PSYCHIC JANE DOHERTY

"The plate makes me feel that it is a part of a set or there is another piece that belongs to it. Maybe, something like a cup to hold coffee, sugar or cream. I don't know what plates like this were used for."

They used them for several things, like in homes when people would come to visit they would place their calling card on it and it may have also been used as you said. However, it was originally a presentation piece and was either presented sometime during the war or after. The inscription is in German and denotes the unit and his front line comrades presented it to him. This came by way of Germany, from the original family, to Argentina and then it found its way into my hands.

"Yes, I can see it used as a place you could put your calling card. I feel it was presented to the soldier as a token of honor. I sense that once it arrived in South America, a woman used it as a small serving tray. Perhaps, the soldier or German family had a connection to the woman who used it in Argentina. The energy around it feels more neutral than emotionally charged. Therefore, it was not used much by the original German owner. It is interesting, yet the energy from it feels OK and if you put it in your hand it almost feels like it is to present something. I could also be picking up that psychically, it was definitely given as an award presentation, as a gift."

CHAPTER 17

TRENCH ART SPRITS

THE CHERRY BLOSSOM NECKLACE AND THE RING

The 1940s Japanese ammunition casings that have been designed to form the links of the chain make this artifact appear to have been professionally produced. Each link was fashioned with a floral design of a cherry blossom stamped onto the surface of each extending oval. If anyone can recall seeing various forms of wartime trench art, they will recall that there have been some items closely resembling fine jewelry. So closely, as a matter of fact, that one might conclude that a jeweler had produced it. This is truly an intriguing conversation piece of history!

PSYCHIC IMPRESSIONS: PSYCHIC JANE DOHERTY

This is considered as trench art and the person who made this had to have plenty of time on their hands. I'm guessing, but considering the workmanship I don't believe it was made in the field, but rather back in Japan.

"Absolutely, I would feel, I was trying to think of what kind of rank or what kind of soldier is like to be waiting to be sent over or waiting to go into action. But they're not. So he's activated but this is what he's doing in the meantime before he's sent over."

It is cherry blossom time with this brass trench art necklace made by a Japanese soldier in his off time. (*Photo Credit – Author's Photo*)

The design seems to have been stamped out by some kind of machine. I believe this was made back at his base in Japan where machines of this type would have been more available.

"I get a 'holding back' feeling. I think the soldier was in active duty, but not deployed yet when he made this piece. He probably created it while still in his country, stationed on a base."

This was made for someone more like a sweetheart, to send or bring home.

"Right, that's what I am feeling, as though it was something that was made for a lover, a sweetheart. I don't feel that he was married; I feel this was for a sweetheart or fiancé, something like that is what this was. I do get a lot of love from it; I get a lot of energy in that sense. I don't feel that this was in battle, it has a very different energy to it, you know, it's more neutral. It's like it's a piece of love and not something connected to battle. That is how I would perceive this. Did the men in Japan wear these?"

No. Soldiers usually made things like this to send home to a girlfriend or wife.

"I do not feel the person who owned this was married. I believe he intended to send it to his lover or bride-to-be. There is a feeling of peace, calm, and a loving energy pulsating from it. It has a different energy field than the other pieces I have held. I think the person who made this was never deployed to another country and never experienced a battle.

What I'm thinking of is this person that made it may have been a jeweler by trade or had been employed by a jewelry firm back in Japan before the war. It is constructed very intricately and had taken him a great deal of time to accomplish this. It is possible that the leaves used could have come pre-shaped, but it may be doubtful if they had that back then."

"You know that it's Japanese because of the cherry blossom design of the stamping. This was either done back at his base in Japan or in a nearby city or possibly his hometown." I don't believe it's gold plated but it's possible, as there seems to be wearing in places, exposing a slight silvery appearance in places on the surface. Also, there are no apparent markings on it."

"What could it be if it was not gold?"

It may be brass as brass can range from a golden color to a silvery one.

"It's not really tarnishing at all, so it's most likely brass, possibly mixed in with copper."

Originally, this WWII brass shell case ring was made by the GI uncle of a young woman and was sent to her grandmother from somewhere in wartime Europe. Eventually, it was passed on to the young woman's mother and then to her after her mother had passed on. Unlike the Japanese necklace in a previous chapter, this ring had been crudely cut and hammered. Nevertheless, it is beautiful in retrospect to the time, place, and conditions under which it had been produced.

PSYCHIC IMPRESSIONS: PSYCHIC JANE DOHERTY

I began by telling Jane that this ring was made from shell casings. When soldiers did not have much to do, they made various items from shell casings, wood, etc. I did not believe that it was German but definitely it was from WWII. It's not the best job on these types of rings that I've seen over the years.

"So you feel that this was not a German soldier who did it?"

No, I don't believe so.

"The first name that comes to mind is 'Bret' or 'Brett' when I hold it. I do not know if this is a German, British or an American name. I believe it is spelled with two t's. Were the British our first allies?"

The British were our allies on the D-day invasion.

"I think it is British. I sense the soldiers waiting before there was action."

This one I know very little about but that on my initial examination of it I received a fair amount of energy from it.

Made for a loved one; this brass trench art ring has a story of its own. (*Photo Credit – Author's Photo*)

Jane continued, "I sense this ring was taken off of a British soldier. I do not feel strong energy emanating from it, which makes me feel he died early in the war. I believe it was taken off of a dead soldier by his comrade. Then it was sent home to his wife or family. The comrade was from the same town as the deceased soldier, so he knew the soldier's family."

CHAPTER 18

HI SAILOR

Anchors Away Mates, hold onto your seats! When I first obtained this WWII United States Navy uniform with the rating of shipfitter (also indicating molder or metalsmith), more affectionately referred to as the "Cracker Jack Navy," very little was known about it. Of WWII vintage and exhibiting the discharge emblem, commonly referred to as "The Ruptured Duck," I was intrigued when I first saw the piggyback orb in the photograph that was sent to me.

After purchasing the uniform several interesting situations began to unfold. While sitting in my office one evening a faint whispering could be heard coming from a closet area. Knowing that others were home at the time I simply brushed it off. The following evening, when no one was at home, I experienced the same faint whispering. The next evening, before retiring, I decided to leave a digital voice recorder activated, making certain to replace the old batteries with fresh ones. Upon awakening the following morning, checking the recorder, the batteries seemed to have been drained after only an hour of so of recording. No EVP was captured, so I felt that it was time for psychic intervention.

PSYCHIC IMPRESSION: MARYANNE VASNELIS

Maryanne began this session by saying that, "I feel that the person who wore this was a young person about eighteen or nineteen years of age with blondish hair and blue eyes. I am seeing

Anchors away with this WWII Navy jumper but this time with a paranormal twist.
(*Photo Credit – Author's Photo*)

ocean and islands, more like in the South Pacific and receiving the names 'Timothy' and 'Mary'."

"This person was in the service a long time; I would say about six to seven years but I am not certain if his service was prior to the war; however, he was one of the first ones called up. When I say 'called up' I feel that it was more of a feeling of his own call to duty, a loyalty of sort and he had enlisted voluntarily. I am not certain if this was before Pearl Harbor or after."

I asked Maryanne if she saw a ship that he may have been involved with and after a deeper concentration she said that, "The only thing coming through is the letter 'W'." So, I decided to push a bit further and I raised a question about battles. Maryanne responded by saying, "I getting a weird country, Indonesia, but from my limited knowledge of the war I am not certain about battles being fought around there but only that he was somehow connected to that area, Indonesia. My feeling is that he was involved in battles but that he always seemed to be coming in at the last minute, like he was not in the center of them but more so coming in near the end of them. I can see him at times firing some sort of machine gun at another ship."

I now jumped a bit and asked Maryanne if she visualized where he was from and her response was, "The name 'Indiana' is coming through." I continued by asking about any women in his life and as Maryanne gave thought to my question, the following information began to come forth, "He had a girlfriend back home but he also had many flings along the way." I interjected the saying "A girl in every port" and Maryanne began to chuckle a bit. Maryanne continued, "Even though he had these flings he felt that he was faithful to his girl back home and that he was never in love with anyone else."

When I asked about his passing, Maryanne responded by saying, "I get the feeling that he did not pass on until way after the war, that at the time he was about forty-five years of age and I am getting the distinct feeling that he did have a family. In a sense he died young. However, I do not see him being wounded during the war but rather I see him passing as a result of stress-related complications related to the war."

CHAPTER 19

A GI'S WOODEN BOX

Still intact is this over sixty year old soldier's box made of wood; empty but only of material things. (*Photo Credit – Author's Photo*)

Now, who would consider purchasing an empty wooden box at an estate sale? I would! I had decided that I would use it to store some of my smaller artifacts. Gazing into the empty box, preparing to place the first artifact into it, something strange happened, a feeling of emptiness came to me (no pun intended) and I decided to make a quick determination, using my pendulum, to see if any latent energy might be present. The box having once belonged to a **WWII GI** from my own state of New Jersey now made it even more interesting for me to find out more about it.

When first receiving this box, I decided to make an attempt to look into the name and address to see if I could make a connection, in the hope that a relative may still be living and residing there but unfortunately I was not successful. Long gone seemed to be the goodies, the souvenirs, that at one time may have been in the box sent home to his mother as are those who possessed this box. Or, did it contain something else, something that psychic intervention may uncover? Was there more of the tale surrounding it? The box may contain more than we ask for!

PSYCHIC IMPRESSIONS: PSYCHIC JANE DOHERTY

Although empty, but still heavy, Jane picked up the box and placed it on her lap. The first thoughts she offered flowed easily from her lips, "This is something a soldier sent home to his family. His belongings were in it. I do not mean clothes, but rather other things he had collected. The objects were keepsakes or souvenirs from WWII. I think one of the articles in the box was something he had taken from a dead German soldier to remind him of his part in defeating the enemy."

CHAPTER 20

THE LETTER

MORE THAN A WARTIME POSTMARK

This WWII German *feldpost* from Amsterdam to an Oberfunker in an officer's home is not unique, save for the fact that this one had an indication of strong latent energy. Can a spirit be connected to a letter? Why not? I am certain that this may also be the case with many of the thousands of wartime letters yet to be discovered. One thing is for certain, that during any wartime period the postal services around the world are flooded with mail, including the U.S. military APO's, German *Feldpost* stations, and other nations' equivalents.

The cover and letter dated December 3rd, 1940, and bearing the return address LO2901-4, Batterie Reserve Flak Abteilung 242, was posted from a unit stationed in Amsterdam (Holland in the Netherlands). This unit was at the time defending the airport near Amsterdam, Schiphol.

PSYCHIC IMPRESSION: PSYCHIC JANE DOHERTY

I began by asking Jane if this person would be a male or a female? "The energy feels light rather than heavy. I interpret the energy to be female." Jane, the word *oberfunker* on the envelope referred to a radio operator. In some of their

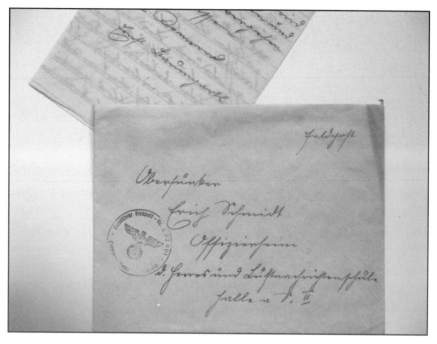

Could this German Fieldpost letter have held some deep, dark secret?
(*Photo Credit – Author's Photo*)

operations, it was not uncommon to find female military communication specialists.

After holding the letter in silence for about a minute, Jane's impression began to emerge. "I feel that this letter was some sort of private communication containing information in 'code'. It was an update on the war, but I feel she could have been a 'spy' trying to arrange a clandestine meeting."

CHAPTER 21

THE MYSTERIOUS MR. H

The old saying "Diamonds are a girls best friend" may be true, however in this case it's sapphires. Since I obtained this unusual silver, sapphire encrusted, and gilded German Luftwaffe pilot award, I have become obsessed with the unusual amount of latent energy and intrigue that seems to surround it. Several scenarios have been speculated by a few of the hierarchy in the field of militaria collecting, offering very little substance as to the artifact's true history.

For any militaria enthusiast, this would be considered a rare find, but to me it was more than that. It became, not just a desire to find its true existence, but a quest to discover its paranormal nexus.

PSYCHIC IMPRESSION: PSYCHIC JANE DOHERTY

"I feel this was a cherished possession of a high-ranking military officer. It was probably presented to him as a special award of some sort. There is a lot of energy coming off of the ring, so I feel the officer wore it for a long time. I see an image of a woman. She probably was the soldier's wife. She took meticulous care of it, because it belonged to her deceased husband. I hear the name Stu or Stuart and it could be the German city, Stuttgart, that I am trying to decipher from the sounds."

Based on my experience, I have found this to be the case involving names or partial names, that the name is that of a city and not the spirit.

PSYCHIC IMPRESSIONS: PSYCHIC LISA PALANDRANO

"When I ask for a name the only thing I'm receiving is the letter 'H'."

Opinion: Since this is truly a special artifact, I have taken both psychic impressions and can reasonably conclude that this piece is of genuine origin, and that it had been presented and worn during the Third Reich period by the individual

A thing of beauty in its own right, this German WWII Luftwaffe variant pilot badge presented an interesting past. Haunted that is! (*Photo Credit – Author's Photo*)

who had received it. That it may either had been found at a location, home, office or command post in or near the German city of Stuttgart, which was located in the American Occupation Zone at the end of WWII or had been removed from the uniform of the recipient by a member of the Allied Forces upon occupation of the city. The letter "H" may have represented the name of the individual who either had confiscated the badge and who had returned from the war with it or the name of the original recipient of the award who may have lived in the city of Stuttgart.

Psychic intervention seems to have played an important part in discovering information that may finally put to rest several of the past suppositions, while confirming others within the militaria collecting community.

Or, does the "H" stand for Hermann Göring?

CHAPTER 22

THE PRODIGAL SON

There are times when surprises come in little packages and this certainly was one of them. At first glance one might ask what the connection between this photograph of a woman and WWII might possibly be? I asked myself the same question. The experience began when I received an unusually strong reaction when holding my pendulum over the photograph. This miniature revealed its surprise when I decided to take it apart to clean the glass. Hidden between the backing cardboard and the front photograph were two additional photographs, one of a soldier in a WWII tan summer uniform and the other of a young child in what appears to be a winter outfit. The photograph of the soldier contained the inscription "The Prodigal Son."

Did the soldier place the inscription there or did the woman write this on the photograph? Who is the child and why where both images tucked away behind the front photograph? I felt that these questions had to be answered so I decided to seek the answers to my questions from one of my psychics, with the hope of additional, revealing, insight as to what may have happened to the soldier.

PSYCHIC IMPRESSION: PSYCHIC JANE DOHERTY

With the three photographs spread before her, Jane placed her hands on top of them and began to concentrate. She immediately

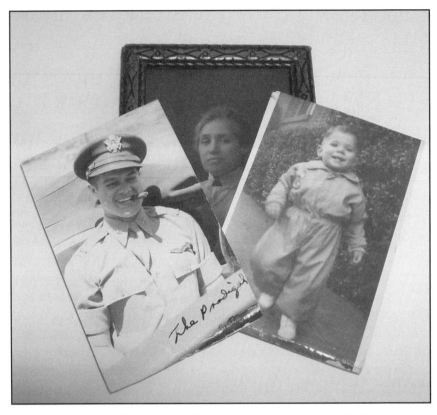

A miniature picture of a mother and two photographs of her prodigal son that were hidden behind her picture. (*Photo Credit – Author's Photo*)

stated that, "I am feeling this woman's sadness and then silence, nothing more was coming through."

I interpreted this as meaning that her son did not return home after the war and that this was the reason for her placing the two photographs behind hers in the frame.

CHAPTER 23

THE HOLOCAUST REVISITED

THE PINK TRIANGLE

S urviving the Nazi Holocaust of the Second World War was this swatch cut from a German KZ camp (concentration camp) inmate's clothing. The pink triangle sewn to it typically identified civilian and military homosexual inmates confined in the various camps throughout Germany and several of the occupied countries during the Nazi reign of terror.

When the Holocaust began, homosexuals were treated with the same venom as the Jews, herded into the concentration camps where the pink triangle was attached to their concentration camp uniform.

Widely regarded as the ultimate symbol of the regime's homophobic paranoia, men who had been denounced as homosexuals before the war had to have this symbol on their outer clothing at all times. It has been estimated that approximately tens of thousands homosexual men were forced to wear this symbol between 1933 and 1944.

Pink triangles were also used for sex offenders such as pedophiles, further associating gays with perverts. The Nazis compelling "undesirable" women, including lesbians, to wear an inverted black triangle, treating women differently.

What makes this one example unique is the paranormal connection to its past. This is not the typical, more common, Star of David, yellow triangle with a pink or other color triangle sewn beneath it, which would have represented a Jewish inmate.

PSYCHIC IMPRESSIONS: PSYCHIC JANE DOHERTY

Jane's immediate feelings were brief and direct. "This person was definitely German, but somehow, the Germans considered him a defiant person. I think he tried to rob them or was considered 'no good' for some reason by the Germans. I believe the soldiers walked through his town and just took him along with everybody else to the concentration camp."

The gruesome reminder of a WWII concentration camp, this swatch that had been cut from an inmate's camp uniform revealed some interesting information about the individual who had worn it. (*Photo Credit – Author's Photo*)

CHAPTER 24

SOLDIER'S ENSEMBLE

What this soldier returned from the war with was some personal items and a few spoons he picked up along the way. (*Photo Credit – Author's Photo*)

When the small box arrived, I really didn't know exactly what to expect to see inside. Even before opening it, I decided to use my pendulum by holding it over the box. Having done this on other occasions, I wanted to see what its general reaction would be. I wasn't disappointed, as the pendulum began to rotate vigorously and almost parallel to the box.

In the box were several items and initially I concluded that the pendulum had been having a cumulative reaction to the latent energy to the artifacts.

PSYCHIC IMPRESSIONS: PSYCHIC JANE DOHERTY

I felt that it would help Jane if she new that these items all belonged to one soldier. However, I told Jane that I had no name for the individual or any other information other than it was bought in an estate sale.

Picking up the cap, Jane said, "Look inside the cap. It is not very worn. It actually looks brand new. I do not feel much energy from it either. I believe the person who wore this died young. He didn't serve more than six months in the service. The spoon from the box has what looks like a letter 'E' scratched on the surface. I am feeling that the letter is for Edward or Edmond. I see Europe in an image, but the region of Belgium, France or Germany. He collected the spoon after killing or capturing an enemy soldier in a home. I think the American soldier lived on the West Coast. I also hear the names Peters, Peterson, and the first name, Lorraine."

CHAPTER 25

MORE THAN JUST HISTORY

PHOTOMONTAGE

A framed photomontage of one man's wartime travels, interesting and with an interesting reveal. (*Photo Credit – Author's Photo*)

Detecting latent energy from the many photographs that comprised this photomontage became a little confusing, as there are many images of individuals in a close-knit environment. This type of situation makes it very difficult for

Detail of previous photo. (*Photo Credit – Author's Photo*)

detailed psychic evaluation. This artifact is genuine WWII period, depicting one man's wartime journey between 1939 and 1945. The name of the individual is known, but exactly where he is located in any of the photographs could not be determined.

PSYCHIC IMPRESSIONS: PSYCHIC JANE DOHERTY

In showing Jane this item, I explained that the names of individuals, dates, and locations were on the reverse side of the matting used to mount the photos and also on the reverse of some of the photos.

Jane's first response was, "Whoever these photos belonged to traveled a great deal. There is a picture of the Taj Mahal, and is this one India or China and the great wall?"

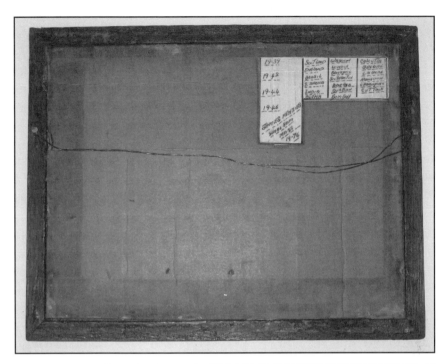

Reverse showing identification of names and places. (*Photo Credit – Author's Photo*) **Right: Detail.**

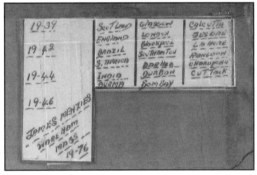

No, that's the Burma Road, I replied.

"Wow, Rangoon, Bombay, Calcutta, Black Pool, London, Glasgow, England, Brazil, South Africa, India, Burma are all pictured here. His name was James Menzies from Wareham, Massachusetts, here on the back. The handwriting is all the same."

Jane concluded the session by saying, "These photos were probably put into this photomontage by the soldier's son. He most likely put it together at a period of time, when James Menzies, his father celebrated a special birthday. It could also have been displayed at a Veterans Day celebration in his hometown, not long after the war had ended."

CHAPTER 26

A PASSPORT TO HEAVEN

Psychic Jane Doherty is holding the scapulars during her evaluation session.
(*Photo Credit – Karen E. Timper, NJGO*)

In wartime, individuals will carry many different and unusual items believed to offer various types of protection; some will survive while others fall. This pair of scapulars was worn by an American G.I. throughout the Second World War and was obtained from his estate. When wearing scapulars, they are worn around the neck from front to rear or they may be carried in ones pocket or elsewhere. No matter where one may carry them, they are believed to offer a heavenly intervention for the individual. The individual who wore this pair was fortunate to have survived the war and never found out if they would have worked for him.

PSYCHIC IMPRESSIONS: PSYCHIC JANE DOHERTY

This session was more about the item itself, as the only impression that came through to Jane was that it once belonged to an American soldier. I decided to include Jane's thoughts about the item as it added to what was previously known about it.

Jane began by saying, "I definitely feel that this came from a monastery."

My question was in the form of a single word, "Originally?"

"Yes, this is an American soldier. I believe that this was gotten in a European monastery. I don't think this was gotten here in the States. I'm very familiar with scapulars and the image of the Blessed Mother is very old and looks to me, you know, to be just European. The idea of wearing a scapular is if that you should die with the scapular you go right to Heaven, so if you didn't get your last rites, if you had this on, it protected you from going to Hell. This is very old and definitely European. I would say Italy or Spain, that's what I feel, probably Italy in a monastery there."

Did this pair of religious scapulars carry this soldier safely through the war? He believed that they did. (*Photo Credit – Author's Photo*)

CHAPTER 27

COMRADES IN BATTLE - COMRADES IN DEATH

This is an example of being able to work directly from flat items scanned and sent by email. After my receiving strong latent energy with my pendulum, I proceeded with a psychic evaluation from the scanned image and many startling pieces of information unfolded during the session.

The discs had been worn into battle by two individuals, who were members of the German elite SS Viking Division, serving, fighting, and dying on the Eastern Front. Both of the discs were dug up in Russia and were located together in a battlefield excavation. In this case, it is important to note that the serial numbers are in sequence; this in itself is an unusual occurrence. They served together and they died together.

PSYCHIC IMPRESSIONS: PSYCHIC JANE DOHERTY

Beginning this session I mentioned to Jane that these items were not mine but were from a well-respected militaria collector, who only wished his initials to be used (G.B.), from Long Island, New York and that he provided the scan of the discs. I only went as far as to include that they were found together.

Jane's first words were, "And they were absolutely ruthless together! I get a much stronger feeling from these then I

Sequential serial numbered SS identification disks. Let the haunting begin! (*Photo Credit – Gaspare Bua*)

received from the gun. (Reference to the Nambu pistol). A gun is simply the instrument that is used to shoot a person. The man who does the killing is simply following orders. However, these discs have a considerable amount of energy around them and I sense a great deal of death associated with them. I believe these two men died together. They were both entrusted with secret information. They had a pact that if one was killed and the other was about to be captured, then he had to kill himself in order to preserve their secrets. They were ruthless in every order they carried out and they killed a lot of people. However, they were close to being captured. They had a dual purpose and they both knew sensitive, secret information. The serial numbers were issued intentionally in order to keep track of the pair. The information they were privy to had to be kept secret at all costs. Therefore, the information had to 'die' with them."

CHAPTER 28

THE SADNESS OF WAR

Horst Haberland is a name I shall not forget. The tragedy and the feelings that this family may have felt was representative of others on all home fronts of the Second World War; the sadness and the kindness. Horst was a young man, serving and dying for his country, for a cause he may or may not have believed in, but he proved his loyalty until the end.

Included in the photograph is his identification book, official death certificate, family's obituary notification card to friends and relatives, and a handwritten letter from his commanding officer.

I received this from my cousin Annemarie in Berlin, Germany, who felt that I should have it because of my interest in military artifacts. Even before opening the package I received a strong reaction from my pendulum. The Haberland family was living in Berlin, as were my cousins, during WWII. The Haberlands ran a tailor shop, which was destroyed, along with their home, by Allied bombs in 1943 and they lost their only son Horst that same year.

After the war, they had moved to Neuglobsow, a little village at the Stechlin Sea. Neuglobsow is about 80 km north of Berlin and during the summers following the war my cousin and her husband Klaus would visit and stay with the Haberlands on weekends. Years later Klaus and Annemarie were able to purchase their own summer home nearby the Haberlands, making their bond of friendship even closer.

When the Haberlands passed on having no surviving relatives, my cousin being executrix of the Haberland estate decided to pass this material on to me. The document is translated below.

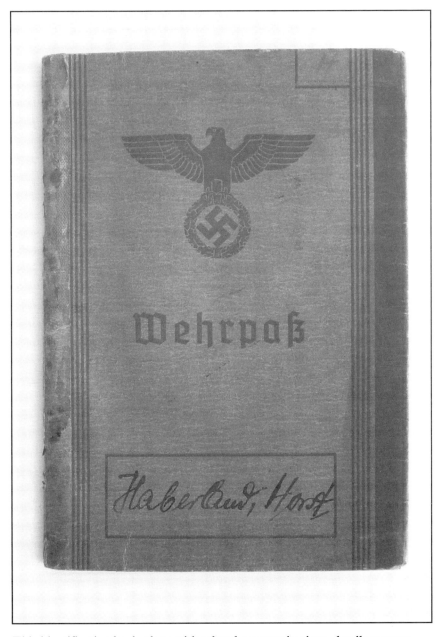

This identification book, along with related communications, details a young German soldier's military career and his short-lived service to the Fatherland. (*Photo Credit – Author's Photo*)

The two page handwritten letter from their son's commanding officer reads:

> As the leader of the company it is my painful duty to tell you that your son, grenadier Horst Haberland was killed in action on October 22.1943. This happened during fights against Slovenian and Italian armed gangs by joining a scouting patrol in Hrzenik, Croatia.
>
> He was always a willing soldier, constantly ready to work and a good comrade and very well liked in the whole company. He fell along with eight comrades of his platoon and he was buried on the cemetery in Krasic (Croatia) where comrades laid him to rest in peace.
>
> We will always keep your son in honorable memory. At the same time I want to express to you, dear Mr. Haberland, my deeply felt sympathy for this hard stroke of fate. Might the thought of your son giving his life for a huge matter, for the freedom of his fatherland soothe the painful loss.
>
> Heil Hitler
>
> H. Kaiser
>
> XX and leader of the company

The death certificate reads:

> Registry Office Berlin Kreuzberg
> Grenadier, tailor Horst Karl Hermann Haberland, Protestant resident in Berlin, Kommandantenstrasse 55 has died in Hrzenik, in the East, October 22.1943.
>
> The deceased was born on 18. May. 1924 in Berlin
> (Registry Office Berlin-Kreuzberg-5a-No.233)
>
> Father: tailor master craftsman Friedrich Karl Haberland
> Mother: Erna Emilie Margarete Haberland nee Schimetzki, both resident in Berlin
>
> Their deceased was not married.
> Berlin, 15. September 1944
> The registrar
> In substituee:
> Free of charge

The obituary card reads:

On 12th of November 1943 we received the unimaginable news that the terrible war took our good-hearted and only son.
Horst Haberland
Born on 18th of May 1924, died on 22nd of October 1943
He rests on a cemetery in Krasic, where comrades laid him to rest in peace.
Asking for quiet sympathy
Karl Haberland and his wife Erna"

The Wehrpass (I.D. book) contains Horst Haberland's personal and complete military record and information.

PSYCHIC IMPRESSIONS: JANE DOHERTY

The following is the only psychic impression that was received and, in itself, is profound in that it details the method by which the life of this young man was taken. It is truly sad that the parents of this boy are no longer with us to share this psychic reveal, as I'm certain that they would have wanted to know how their son had actually met his young and untimely end.

"I believe he was blown-up. I can see bits and pieces of metal flying in different kinds of directions. This was probably pieces of shrapnel. I believe this happened in an area where several countries were represented by soldiers."

CHAPTER 29

THE LOCKET

This locket came from the German estate of SS Standartenfuhrer Hermann Barth, along with many artifacts once belonging to Reichsmarschall Hermann Göring and his wife Emmy. This ninety-year-old locket has on the front the engraved initials EG and on the back the initials LK, which were her former husband's initials when she was married to German film producer Ludwig Karl Köstlin. Emma Johanna Henny "Emmy" Sonnemann-Göring was born 24 March 1893, became an actress, and the second wife of Hermann Göring. Emmy Göring was born in Hamburg, Germany to a wealthy salesman and was an actress at the National Theatre in Weimar. She became Emmy Köstlin upon her marriage to actor Karl Köstlin in late 1916, but they later divorced.

Hermann Barth was a close friend of the Reichsmarschall and the Göring's, as well as Reichsführer SS Heinrich Himmler. Barth was responsible for the SS Education School in Berlin during WWII.

Among the artifacts in his estate were many personal and private items of the Görings. Exactly how Barth came into possession of this locket and the other items is not known and may never be. However, given the friendship between him and the Göring family, I can only speculate that they may have either been gifts or he had somehow been able to save some of the Göring's treasured artifacts. Other items in the estate were many letters from Göring and Himmler, antlers (Göring was an avid hunter), goblets, porcelain ... and this locket.

The following is a quote from *Time Magazine*, Monday, June 25, 1945:

Paranormally charged silver locket once belonging to Emme Göring, wife of WWII German Reichsmarschall Hermann Göring. (*Photo Credit – Author's Photo*)

Emmy Sonnemann Göring arrived last week at Neustadt, near Nuremburg. She was riding in a Mercedes Benz. A two-and-a-half-ton truck followed with a month's supply of food, quantities of clothing, and jewelry. In her party were her seven-year-old daughter Edda, a German Lieutenant Colonel (Colonel), and his orderly. Two officers of the U.S. 19th Infantry Division, said a *New York Times* Dispatch, the Lieutenant Colonel presented an order from an unnamed SHAEF Major General, requesting that Frau

Goering be given all assistance. U.S. Soldiers obediently helped Frau Göring, her daughter, and nursemaid move into one of the Göring's many villas.

The German officer may have been Barth who, on several later occasions, may have been permitted to visit Emmy Göring at the villa.

Emmy Göring was in Neustadt-Nuremburg with her husband, Reichsmarschall Hermann Göring, up until the end, when, as a convicted war criminal, he cheated the hangman's noose and committed suicide on October 15, 1946, the night before he was to be hanged. This seemed to be a fitting end for one of the most flamboyant personalities in the Third Reich.

Open locket showing the inner compartment in which either a lock of hair or a photograph may have been placed. (*Photo Credit – Author's Photo*)

The locket is made of silver and exactly what it contained when worn by Emmy is a mystery and will most likely remain one; unless it can eventually be discovered through deep psychic intervention.

PSYCHIC IMPRESSIONS: PSYCHIC JANE DOHERTY

Holding the locket tightly in her hand, Psychic Jane Doherty asked, "and this opens?"

I immediately responded to her question with a "yes" and proceeded to show her how it opens.

Jane immediately asked, "Why do I keep getting a lock of hair?" Jane was asking this to herself but out loud.

I explained that was what lockets of this type usually held and sometimes a photograph. What is missing is the circular piece of rounded cover glass.

"I feel like saying 'royalty' but my feeling is more like some sort of high, like the wife of a high ranking individual."

I could not hold my enthusiasm any longer and felt compelled to let Jane know how incredibly accurate her feeling was! I then told her the details of the entire scenario of the artifact, just as you read in the opening of this chapter.

Since there was no actual spirit communication I felt that Jane's comments were sufficient, as I already had known all that was necessary about this locket. However, I was hoping that a spirit connection would have been made. Possibly this may yet happen in another session.

CHAPTER 30

THE SWORD

This artifact is a First World War sword of Imperial Germany that was taken as a souvenir by Otto H. Rust, who was a member of the U.S. 7th Field Artillery during the Second World War. I wish to thank his two sons, Thomas and James, for giving me their permission to investigate this artifact and to use the information provided on behalf of their father, Otto, who is still with us. The 7th Field Artillery Regiment participated in the amphibious assault landing in Algeria as part of Operation Torch. After fighting across North Africa, the regiment participated in 1st Infantry Division's assault of Omaha Beach.

This type of sword was worn by staff officers and may have been worn by the same officer serving in the Second World War if he had been an officer in WWI as well. In retrospect, the officer may have risen in rank to that of general either before the Second World War, sometime during it or was already a general in WWI.

PSYCHIC IMPRESSIONS: PSYCHIC LISA PALANDRANO

Lisa's initial impression was, "I don't pick up very much. What I'm picking up is more than one owner, two actually. Its been around awhile, mostly just for show. I do get the word blood, so it might have seen some action. It was saved by the first owner, who kept it till he died and now I believe it's with its second owner."

In a note sent to one of Otto's sons, I included Lisa's impressions and the following commentary.

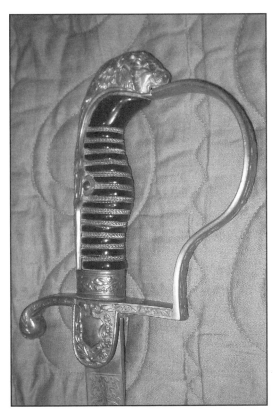

This German Imperial Officer Sword was taken from what was believed to be a sleeping general but turned out to be one who had crossed over. (*Photo Credit – Thomas Rust*)

I believe that what Lisa is referencing here is that the "first owner" would be the German and that the "second owner" would be Otto Rust. What is key here is that we have to find out if this sword was taken on the battlefield from a dead German. Should this be the case, then the "word blood" and "It was saved by the first owner, who kept it till he died" would fit the scenario. He would have kept it from the First World War, being that it's an Imperial German sword, all through WWII or at least up until he was killed (died).

The initial response from the son of the sword's present owner:

"Richard, this is very interesting. What you say makes sense to me. The sword is virtually unblemished so I can envision a scenario where my father could be identified as the second owner. We understand through my father that he picked up the sword from the general, who was lying dead in a jeep. He expired from the repercussion of a bomb, my father tells the story that describes the general as appearing asleep without any outward signs of a mortal wound...Tom."

CHAPTER 31

MYSTERY OF THE WALKING STICK

Surviving for the past sixty-plus years, this walking stick was from the Hermann Göring estate at Carinhall and later in the possession of Alfred Stöhr, then a young SS man barely eighteen years of age who, first serving with the 11th Waffen-SS Education Regiment at Nuremburg, later was assigned as a personal SS guard of Adolf Hitler at the Obersalzberg in Berchtesgaden. Earlier he had served a short time on the front with the 8th Waffen-SS Cavalry Division.

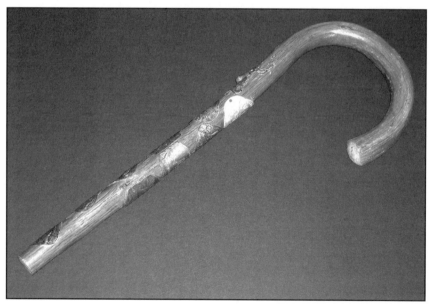

Close-up looking at the area where the cut was made to shorten the length of the walking stick. (*Photo Credit – Author's Photo*)

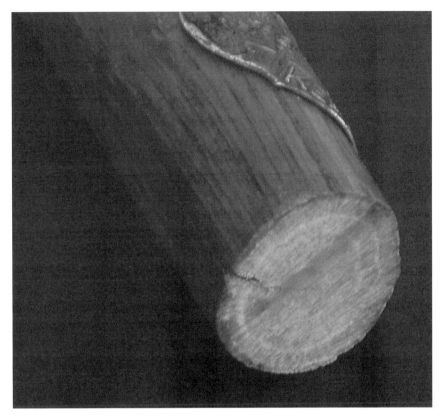

Close-up looking at the area where the cut was made to shorten the length of the walking stick. (*Photo Credit – Author's Photo*)

The walking stick is made of German oak, the national tree of Germany. It was most likely from the Obersalzberg-Berchtesgaden area located in the German Bavarian Alps and for an unknown reason, had been mysteriously cut from the original size to fourteen and one half inches long. I cannot think a reason for this with the exception of limited space transporting it.

Affixed are ten vintage and rare badges circling the walking stick, a deer with the engraved words Obersalzberg that was the area of Adolf Hitler and Hermann Göring's estates. Below the deer is a Munich Hofbräuhaus badge, the Purtschellerhaus, St. Bartholomä, Almbachklamm, and the Kehlsteinhaus, also known as the Eagle's Nest, is a chalet-style building which when built was an extension of the Obersalzberg complex built by the Nazis in the German

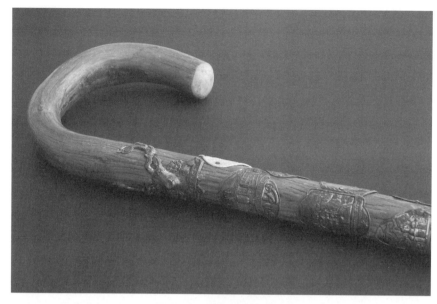

Close-up of upper, main section of the walking stick. (*Photo Credit – Author's Photo*)

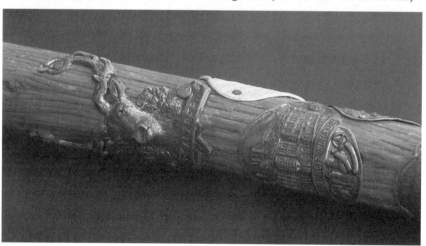

Detail of previous photo. (*Photo Credit – Author's Photo*)

Alps near Berchtesgaden. The Kehlsteinhaus was an official 50th birthday present for Adolf Hitler. On the backside are four badges depicting Innsbruck, Zugspitze Münchner Haus, Kaiser Wilhelm Denkmal – Porta Westfalica, Kitzbühl Tirol. Evidently, the original owner of this walking stick was an avid hunter.

Herman Göring was not only Reichs Home Secretary but also a hunter, and on July 3, 1934, his new "Reichsjägdgesetz" (Reichs hunting law) became legal. It arranged all hunters in hierarchical groups. The so called "Jägermeister" (master hunter) existed already during the Baroque period. Göring recalled that and appointed, in 1934, the first "kreis and gau-jägermeister," with himself on top of the pyramid, as the "Reichsjägermeister."

It is not surprising that an indication of latent energy has been detected surrounding this artifact when you consider those who once owned it. Were we able to discover why it was cut? Regrettably, so many people have handled this walking stick over the years that the possibility of forensic identification of latent fingerprints, or other remnants of DNA that may have remained on its surface from those who had early on possessed it, may no longer be possible.

There is one possibility. The rusting nails holding the various metal badges to the walking stick may have, because of the rust coating, recorded past events. When the conditions are right these nails may give up information in the form of a residual projection. This type of projection was described in detail in an earlier chapter.

PSYCHIC IMPRESSIONS: PSYCHIC JANE DOHERTY

I began by asking Psychic Jane Doherty about the artifact having been cut.

"I get a sense this stick was cut so that it could be displayed on a wall or in a case once it was no longer used as a walking stick. I think it was given as a testament of 'honor' or 'loyalty'. There are metal badges on the stick. I think these badges are there to remember accomplishments or as some sort of memorabilia."

What follows now becomes more profound then I had ever imagined!

"It has a deeper significance. It was not just cut. I feel it had a symbolic meaning or it was presented as an accolade of some sort. I am seeing a man who has close, daily contact with Hitler. This man is probably who owned the walking stick."

As Jane continued, I became even more enthused about the find that I had made.

"I believe this stick was given to the owner by Hitler. Then he passed it on to another individual. It was cut afterwards. It was splintered below the point where the metal pieces were attached. The upper portion was then kept as a memento. The new owner did not use it as a walking stick, but rather as an item the owner displayed for memories."

I asked Jane if it is possible that some of the feelings that you are getting were residual.

"Yes, yes!"

My reason for asking this is that I noticed that some of the tiny nails holding the metal badges in place are rusted. For how long I can't say and there is considerable tarnishing or possible rusting appearance to some of them.

"There is a lot of energy surrounding this, when I hold it. I also see visions of a man walking through wooded areas and using it to clear brush as he walked."

I next asked Jane if she saw any colors, colors of uniforms.

"I see dark blue. It's a dark color blue and what stands out ever more is that I see a lot of decorations on the uniform."

I now decided to tell Jane that Hermann Göring was quite close to Hitler and that he wore blue uniforms. That he was the head of the German Luftwaffe and that he was a very flamboyant individual. I felt that this might be a connection to its original owner.

At this point I told Jane about the individual's wife, whom I received this artifact from, and that she had kept this because Hitler himself may have given this to her husband directly or to someone close to Hitler.

More unfolded as Jane continued, "I keep getting it is connected to Hitler in some way and that is why the walking stick was kept for such a long time. It almost signifies a love or a special bond that her husband had with Hitler. His wife also kept it special in her heart, not that it just belonged to her husband but because of the fact of the kinship with Hitler."

PSYCHIC IMPRESSIONS: PSYCHIC MARYANNE VASNELIS

During a session with Psychic Maryanne Vasnelis some of the information gained through Psychic Jane Doherty was confirmed, giving me a closer correlation of what had previously been known of this artifact.

When Maryanne held this walking stick in her hand she immediately sensed the strong latent energy that I had previously experienced with the use of my pendulum.

"Gerald, Jerry, Gerhard" were the names that immediately came to Maryanne followed by a feeling of Switzerland. My response to her was that she was close, that it was from Bavaria. Her feelings that followed were that it was somehow important family-wise but that it had a history and had become sort of a family heirloom.

Although the walking stick seemed to exhibit a life of its own, Maryanne began hearing that the spirit who was connected to the walking stick was in the military. She had the vision of him in a greenish color uniform and then in a blue one and that it was a good luck symbol to the person who had received this from its original owner but that it wasn't used as a walking stick, being more of a good luck thing to hold onto.

Lastly, Maryanne received the name "FAUST" as another spirit who may have been passing on this information. It (the walking stick) has a lot of good memories attached to it (I believe this is referencing the hunting adventures of the original owner or many pleasant walks through the Bavarian countryside).

Note: Is it possible that this may have been partially residual as the tiny nails affixing the various metal tags to the walking stick have rusted over the years and the plating of the tags' finish has tarnished from time?

CHAPTER 32

A SOLDIER'S V-MAIL LETTER TO JENNIE

During the latter years of World War II, V-Mail became a popular way to correspond with a loved one serving overseas. V-Mail letters were written on forms that could be purchased at five and ten cent stores or at the post office. These special forms were photographed, put on film, flown across the world, and then reproduced at the mail center closest to the recipient's position. The development of the V-Mail system reduced the time it took a soldier to receive a letter by a month – from six weeks by boat to twelve days or less by air. However, the main advantage of V-Mail was its compact nature. Reduction in the size and weight of the letters translated into more space for crucial military supplies on cargo planes; one advertisement explained that 1,700 V-Mail letters could fit in a cigarette packet, while reducing the weight of the letters in paper form by 98%. Transport of the letters by plane minimized the chances that the enemy would intercept the letters, although writers were reminded to delete any information that might prove useful to the enemy in case some V-Mail was captured. Americans on the home front were encouraged by the government and private businesses to use V-Mail. Letters from home were compared to "a five minute furlough," and advertisements that instructed how, when, and what to write in a V-Mail reached a peak in 1944. Letters were to be cheerful, short, and frequent. V-Mail made it possible for servicemen halfway across the world to hear news from home on a weekly basis.

The above information was compiled from Duke University Libraries Digital Collections.

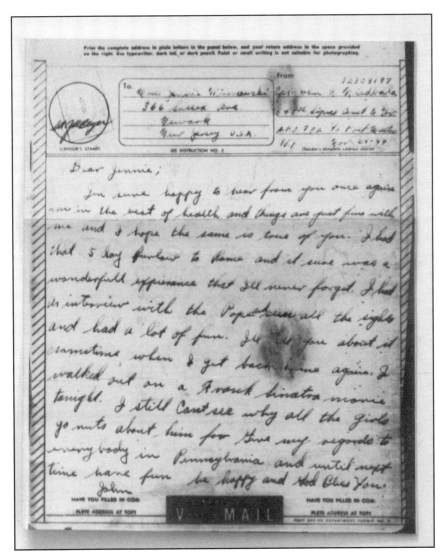

One of the many thousands of V-Mail letters that were prominent during WWII. These were letters either written by a service man to someone on the home front or by a loved one writing to someone in the service. Written on a special form that was reduced by photomechanical means to save space.
(*Photo Credit – Author's Photo*)

Written November 24, 1944, John, the soldier who sent this letter to his sweetheart Jennie, was with the U.S. 549th Signal Construction Company and what is most interesting about this "Letter to Jennie" is his mentioning of his five day furlough to Rome, having an interview with Pope Pius XII, and his walking out on a movie that starred wartime singing idol Frank Sinatra, writing that, "I still can't see why all the girls go nuts about him for."

Besides the latent energy surrounding this letter, the door of memories seemed to crack open a little for me. I was young, only nine years old at the time, but recall many letters of this type that my family members and neighbors received from their loved ones in the service during this time period. On the home front, it was not uncommon for family members to write their loved ones on the battlefront on a daily basis. Some would wait, sitting on their porches, for the postman to come each day for that long-awaited letter to arrive. During those war years we had two mail deliveries each day, one in the morning and another in the afternoon.

PSYCHIC IMPRESSIONS: PSYCHIC JANE DOHERTY

To Psychic Jane Doherty this artifact was obviously a letter or note. Therefore, I explained to her what it was and that initially I had picked up some latent energy from it. I felt that in this case I should do this psychic investigation, and also with similar types of letters.

"I feel that the reason why you received energy from the letter is that the man who had written it did not come back from the war. That he died in the war."

Jane did not receive any additional feelings so we closed the session.

CHAPTER 33

THE COCONUT SPIRIT

This was a unique message sent to the Steins from their son, who was serving with the United States Forces on the war-torn island of New Guinea in the South Pacific in 1944. Unusual, yes, one-of-a-kind, possibly, but what makes this one different is the message from within or would it be more appropriate to say from without or the other side?

The campaign on New Guinea is all but forgotten, except by those who served there. Battles with names like Tarawa, Saipan, and Iwo Jima overshadow it. Yet Allied operations in New Guinea were essential to the U.S. Navy's drive across the Central Pacific and to the U.S. Army's liberation of the Philippine Islands from Japanese occupation.

To present a snapshot of what this sailor and others may have had to endure on this, the second largest island in the world: disease thrived on New Guinea. Malaria was the most debilitating, but dengue fever,

A coconut that traveled across the wartime Pacific Ocean to the East Coast of New York, adding a bit of paranormal lightness from those connected to it. (*Photo Credit – Author's Photo*)

129

Close-up of the coconut's main, painted design. (*Photo Credit – Author's Photo*)

dysentery, scrub typhus, and a host of other tropical sicknesses awaited unwary soldiers in the jungle. Scattered, tiny coastal settlements dotted the flat malarial north coastline, but inland the lush tropical jungle swallowed men and equipment.

Possibly by sending this coconut, unwrapped, addressed to his parents was his way of lightening the mood of the time, place, and situation in which he had found himself. Different, but nevertheless it reminds me of the coconut that our former President John F. Kennedy had written a desperate rescue message upon when his boat, the PT-109 that he was commanding, was destroyed in this same South Pacific Theater of Operations, by Japanese gunfire, during the Second World War.

I could hardly wait to discover what may be connected to this artifact and when it finally came into my possession I immediately examined it with my pendulum. The latent energy field was strong and, once again, I could not wait for one of my psychics to do a hands-on evaluation.

PSYCHIC IMPRESSIONS: MARYANNE VASNELIS

Holding the coconut with both hands, Maryanne's first thoughts were that it said New Guinea on it, but that origin was someplace else, nearby but not exactly there. She next received the name of "Joe" but that the person who found this was not the person who wound up with it.

Revealed next was that the person who stumbled upon it thought that it would be "cool" to keep but it ended up being passed to somebody else. She felt that the first individual who had it died later in the war, however, he had passed it on before he did, feeling that it would make a good "gag" gift.

More information began to emerge as Maryanne received a second name of "Jim" and reiterated that the earlier name of Joe was the first person that had the coconut. That this was both a gag and friendship gift at the same time to send home.

Close-up of the postal sender and recipient addresses of this unusual gift.
(*Photo Credit – Author's Photo*)

CHAPTER 34

ONE - TWO - BUTTON MY SHOE

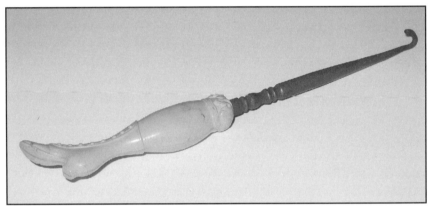

This high-top shoe button hook is from the early part of the twentieth century and has a significant personal paranormal connection to me.
(*Photo Credit – Author's Photo*)

I know, I know, and realizing that this artifact has no direct connection to wartime, with the only exception being that it has survived through several wartime periods and that it will always remain a part of our family. I felt that this deserved a place in my book since it was my mother that, from the other side, had a part in the pendulum that I use coming to me at the time that it did. I remember, as a child, this shoe buttonhook was once part of a complete dresser ensemble, most of which did not survive, with this being the exception.

The only other connection is that both my mother's parents were from Germany and my grandfather, before immigrating to the United States, was an Officer in the Royal Prussian Army during the early 1860s, whom I mentioned in the dedication of my book.

This early 1900s high-button shoe hook is a personal item that belonged to my mother from the time that she was a young girl, one of the few very personal items, beside the many photographs and memories, of hers that I have. This still carries much of her energy, something that I have felt for many years, even before I became involved in the paranormal.

My mother, a truly wonderful, giving person, was born in 1899 and passing in 1975 at the age of seventy-six. On occasion I experience visitations from both her and my dad in dreams and my oldest daughter Karen has had similar dreams of them, dreams mirroring mine.

PSYCHIC IMPRESSIONS: PSYCHIC MARYANNE VASNELIS

This session quickly and surprisingly turned into an unexpected psychic reading and nothing about the shoe buttonhook. Seemingly, the artifact was simply a trigger to what followed.

Startling and quick was Maryanne's first reaction, asking me, "Who is Margaret, to say hi from Margaret?"

My reply was equally as fast, that Margaret was my mother's middle name. Maryanne continued, saying that she's laughing at what you're doing, that if you went back in years you would be doing nothing like what you're doing now. She's talking about the second part of what you do, the paranormal part. She would never have pictured you doing anything like this, that it is far from any "realm" that she would ever imagine you would be into.

Your mother is now telling me that she is with a baby. This reference is not clear, as she did not have a baby that passed. Repeating this, your mother is saying that she is with a young child, that she wants you to know this, and that she is with the children. The reference here is either to my children or my grandchildren.

What is believed to be an unrelated intervention by another spirit, Maryanne received the name of "Patsy." I could not make any connection to this name.

As the communication continued, another revelation came forth, "Your mother is saying that she or you got it in the mail, that she loved it because the surface is so smooth, that she could keep it in her hand. Your mother here is taking about the wood cross, the one you use as a pendulum. It came from a ministry that she associated with, that she had attended church a lot when she was here.

"Your mother is now showing me 'Indian feathers'." I knew of no connection to this.

"Your mother is telling me that she visits a lot and that she is with you and a young man about nineteen or twenty years old, that she travels between the three of you. The reference here seems to be my daughter Karen and her son Keith Jr. or possibly my granddaughter Krissy."

Nearing the conclusion of this unexpected session and in reference to Krissy, my mother sees another female with her.

CHAPTER 35

CRASH AND BURN

This German WWII award was presented to an individual utilizing small arms fire to down an enemy aircraft, single-handed. (*Photo Credit – Author's Photo*)

K nown by its German name, *Tieffligervernichtungsabzeichen* (Special badge for shooting down Low Flying Aircraft, utilizing only small arms weapons (1945)), the badge is comprised of a blackened metal plane on a silver cloth strip with two black stripes for shooting down one aircraft. There is no set monetary value as only twenty-seven allegedly were ever awarded. This same badge was awarded with a gilt metal plane on a gold cloth strip with two black stripes for shooting down a fifth aircraft. There is also no set value as none were thought to ever have been awarded.

Originally from an unknown German estate, it signifies a single act of bravery performed by this soldier. Eventually finding its way to the United States into a thirty-year collection on the West Coast, this rare cloth sleeve patch has not often been seen since very few had ever been presented or have genuine examples emerged from this wartime period. This example was a veteran's bring-back, where and how he obtained it is not known as the veteran's estate knew nothing about it.

PSYCHIC IMPRESSIONS: LISA PALANDRANO

Psychic Lisa Palandrano received a brief impression that the individual who had been presented with this badge had used a machine gun to down the aircraft. He was hurt that his badge had been "stolen" from him later in the war.

PSYCHIC IMPRESSIONS: MARYANNE VASNELIS

This was one of those instances where psychic impressions bordered on receiving slightly comical information from a spirit. When Psychic Maryanne Vasnelis held this object she sensed two men.

With a smile on her face Maryanne said that she had immediately received the name "Tiny Tim" and that she saw two men, a tall man with a short partner. The short man was referring to his tall partner as "Tiny Tim," being his nickname because of his height. The short spirit indicated that the badge belonged to his tall partner, who was with him. The reference is believed to be to when the act of shooting down the plane occurred.

Maryanne now received the name of "Hans Hoffer" or "Hoffman," ending the communication.

CHAPTER 36

WARTIME SMOKES

THE MYSTERIOUS TWIN

One of the American G.I.'s favorite sayings was, "Hey mack, got a smoke?" This is an interesting story about a cigarette pack, its wartime connection, and the extended trip that it made.

During the Second World War, my father was employed by a firm in Newark, New Jersey, and one of his fellow workers, a young man in his early twenties, received the proverbial "Greetings From The President Of The United States." Shortly after receiving his call to duty in late 1943, he was off to unknown destinations and hoping but not knowing if he would ever return.

Now, the men in the shop wanted to do something to show that they were thinking of him, so they all chipped in the enormous sum of three dollars, the total cost back then of two cartons of his favorite cigarettes and sent them off to him. The package began its journey at the United States Post Office in Newark, New Jersey, and was diverted to many wartime locations before finally catching up with the soldier. When it finally did catch up with him, he had been killed in action and now the package began its return journey back home to Newark, New Jersey, to the men who were thoughtful enough to send it.

The package made its round trip journey, returning almost one year later in late 1944. The two cartons of cigarettes were split among the shop employees and this is the one pack that my father had brought home, keeping it until he passed away in 1985. I'm just glad that he had kept this all those years and that I am privileged to have it, along with the memories.

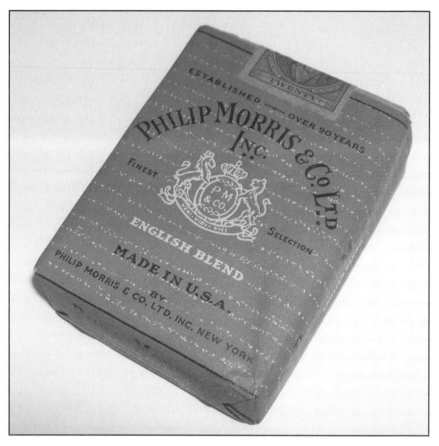

Cigarette pack of 1940s vintage, a time when a carton of cigarettes sold for the enormous price of $1.50. (*Photo Credit – Author's Photo*)

One day my son located the pack of cigarettes among my fathers possessions, tore it open, and took one of the cigarettes from it. I only discovered this years later. When I discussed this with him, I was told the reason why he had only taken one cigarette from the pack was that when he lit it, it had burned down quite rapidly and he had only gotten three puffs from it. He had not realized that tobacco that old would have dried out considerably, even though it was in a sealed package. A lesson learned.

As one might imagine, the latent energy surrounding this artifact is high and when I presented it to my psychics for their impressions, other than what is obvious, nothing was told of the purpose or the long journey.

PSYCHIC IMPRESSIONS: PSYCHIC MARYANNE VASNELIS

Maryanne began by expressing a slightly confused reaction that somehow this cigarette pack was, in some strange way, connected to stopping a bullet.

Profound as it may seem, the twist to the above voyage of this pack of cigarettes would not have been possible without psychic intervention. Maryanne's first reaction was indeed a bit eerie in that she saw and felt a bullet hole in it when there was none visible. She wondered if the individual has saved this pack of cigarettes to remember? She began to envision that this cigarette pack somehow saved the life of the individual because the bullet did not go entirely through it.

Note: My knowing the story about this artifact leads me to believe that paranormal intervention occasionally steps in and in this situation the combination of this cigarette pack and an identical one crossed paths. The serviceman who the two cartons of cigarettes were sent to was the brand he had smoked and logic would dictate that he had a similar (twin) pack of this brand in his pocket at the time he met his demise.

CHAPTER 37

THE SILENT KILLER

This Civil War bayonet presents a unique story, one that waited patiently for 150 years to be revealed. (*Photo Credit – Richard Wisenfelder, NJGO*)

During September 2007, John Wisenfelder and his son Kenny, both avid Civil War buffs, were visiting a few of the Civil War battlefields while on their vacation. Their travels included two of the National Parks of Gettysburg, Pennsylvania, and Antietam, which is located just outside of Sharpsburg, Maryland. It was not too far outside of Antietam when they saw a spot in a small open area on the road surrounded by a clump of very old trees and a few picnic benches that were being shaded by the trees so they decided to stop, have lunch, and rest a while.

After lunch, John had taken notice to a very old tree stump that seemed to be hiding behind some brush. Carefully inspecting the stump, John noticed a large hole in its side. Hesitating for a moment, he decided to reach into the dark hole. Filled with anticipation, he put his hand into the hole, felt something hard and cold, and pulled out a Civil War bayonet.

This artifact had been brought to my attention at one of our meetings by Rich Wisenfelder, a member of my daughter's paranormal group. He sat there quietly holding it wrapped in a towel for the first part of the meeting. When the opportunity to take a break came, he said that he had something really interesting to show me. Although not of Second World War vintage, this artifact and the circumstances surrounding its discovery were so unique that I would have been remiss if I had not included it in my book. Items such as this, from the period it was from, are rarely found in this completely intact condition.

At this point I feel that I should tell you that both he and his uncle are avid users of metal detectors and have discovered many unusual artifacts on their ventures; however, this is probably their most interesting and historic find.

Unwrapping the object very carefully, what unfolded before my eyes was truly unique, a long metal object, blackened and pock marked from age, that was slightly over one foot in length and tapered to a point at one end. I immediately knew that this was a bayonet but not resembling one from the Second World War. He told me that it was from the Civil War and that his uncle had discovered it on the outskirts of Antietam, but not within the national park boundaries.

Now, my paranormal curiosity was raised and he went on with the story of how this unique artifact had been discovered. While walking near an old tree stump his uncle's metal detector began to beep loudly and rapidly. Discovering a hollow near the bottom of the stump, he placed

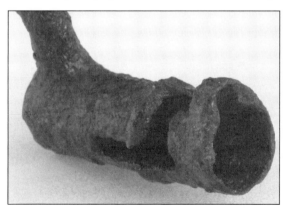

Close-up of bayonet socket section for fitting it to a musket. (*Photo Credit – Richard Wisenfelder, NJGO*)

his hand into the hole, which was near the ground level and felt an object. One can imagine the feeling he experienced when out came this bayonet.

Was it from the South or from the Union Army? Was there latent energy surrounding it? We now had to find out more about it and fortunately I had brought my pendulum to the meeting. Holding it over the artifact, it immediately began to rotate. My first words were "you're in luck tonight as we have a new member, Maryanne Vasnelis, who is a psychic."

When Maryanne came back into the room, I asked her if she would hold the artifact and give her impressions. Being told nothing about it other that that the object was a bayonet, she provided the following information.

PSYCHIC IMPRESSIONS: PSYCHIC MARYANNE VASNELIS

Maryanne's first thought was Civil War, "I get the name Gettysburg, that this was once in the possession of a soldier of the South who also acted as a northerner" (referring to the Union Army). I'm receiving the name John Tyler and the name New Jersey, that he was from there."

I did ask Maryanne if any numbers had come to mind and she immediately replied, "that when I had finished my question the number 427 flashed before her."

Now, the juices of curiosity began to flow and Richard's quest for more information had begun. He started his research based on the information that our psychic, Maryanne, was able to provide. One must keep in mind that the Mason Dixon Line came very close to the state of New Jersey and that it would have been possible for John Henry to have easily switched to the side of the Southern States and that at one point, due to certain unforeseen circumstances, he may have switched his loyalty to the Northern States Union Army.

CHAPTER 38

TWO SHIPS PASSING IN THE NIGHT

This beautiful solid silver signet ring was found, as many such items are, by an individual on an excursion to a flea market in Flint, Michigan, in a box containing other wartime military items. Originally, the items in the box were purchased at an estate sale.

Silver signet ring was a gift of remembrance but turned out to be a forget me ring instead. (*Photo Credit – Author's Photo*)

Taking a step back in time for a moment, it is now Austria 1945-1946 and Margit wanted her soldier to remember her. By giving him this ring engraved with her name she felt that he would never forget her. Who was this soldier, who was Margit, and did he remember? Or, could it be that this military man took a well deserved leave at Margit Island, or Margaret Island in the middle of the Danube River (Margitsziget, Budapest, Hungary) and simply wished to record his visit there by engraving the names and dates into the ring? If so, then why would the name Austria instead of Hungary be engraved inside? Another twist to this puzzle is that the name Margit is also Norwegian. At first many unanswered questions entered my mind, but let us find out together as we travel this paranormal path. The latent energy connected to this ring is unusually strong, a good indicator that it has a story to tell.

PSYCHIC IMPRESSIONS: PSYCHIC MARYANNE VASNELIS

The feelings from Maryanne Vasnelis were confirming and added a new twist to the path of this ring.

At first glance the initials engraved on the face of the ring seemed a bit confusing and could be read several ways because of the way that the overlapping letters seem to have been engraved. The engraving on the inside of the ring was a different story and to Maryanne it was clearly the name of the town Margit, where the American soldier and a female friend had first met. This relationship became much clearer as the session progressed.

Maryanne had the feeling that the ring had been given to the woman, but then was returned to the soldier. Even though the ring was not made for a woman, it was given as a token, something to remember him by. However, the feeling was that, somehow, this ring had passed through the mail back to the soldier after he had returned to America.

Engraving and silver mark on the inside of the ring. (*Photo Credit – Author's Photo*)

Not seeing anyone still having a connection to the ring, a vision of the initials EDA or DOA flashed before her. Immediately following was the feeling that this soldier had married shortly after returning home; however, he did have a girlfriend overseas and left her behind after the war.

Maryanne continued feeling that she could not understand why the girl had returned the ring, since most necessities of life were in scarce supply after the war and she would have had a need for money and could have sold the ring. "I can't understand why she would send the ring back."

Similar scenarios were common after the Second World War and as Maryanne so aptly put it, "The girlfriend and the soldier never connected again, like two ships passing in the night."

CHAPTER 39

IN THE SPIRIT OF BANZAI

Many years ago my son-in-law showed me some Second World War artifacts that he had come upon, one was this Japanese Samuri Katana sword. At the time my interest was strictly with the historical and militaria aspect; my interest in the paranormal had not yet been tweaked.

For collectors of WWII Japanese militaria, the Samurai sword is one of the most sought after military antiques. Its popularity in the movies and television has helped propelled it into the status of a popular icon. The strength, simplicity, and beauty of the blade have made it a legend.

I felt it most fitting to title this chapter "In the Spirit of Banzai" as Banzai" is a Japanese cheer that translates as "Long life!" or "Hurrah!" It is usually repeated three times to express enthusiasm, celebrate a victory, applause and favor on happy occasions while raising both arms. This cheer is commonly made together with the large group of people. People unfamiliar with the Japanese language seem to confuse "Banzai" with a war cry. This is common because the Japanese soldiers shouted "Tennouheika

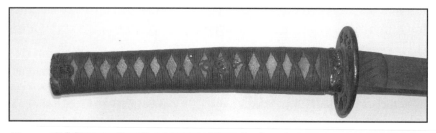

Close-up of the sword's grip and tang. (*Photo Credit – Author's Photo*)

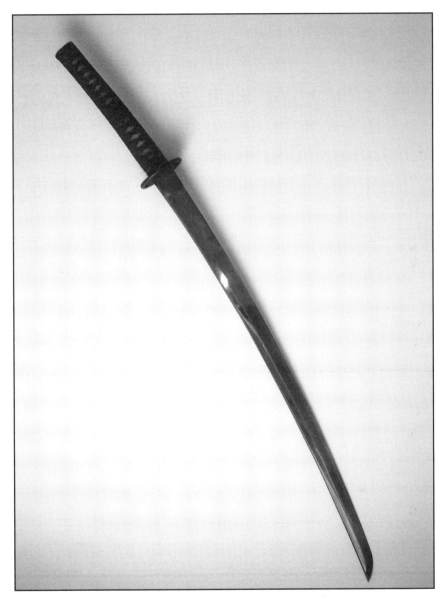

A rare Japanese WWII Katana sword, which remains complete with its sheath (not shown here) and military identification. (*Photo Credit – Author's Photo*)

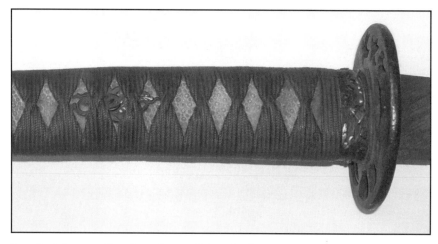

Detail of the sword's grip and tang. (*Photo Credit – Author's Photo*)

Banzai!" when they were dying during World War II. In this context what they meant was "Long live the Emperor" or "Salute the Emperor."

PSYCHIC IMPRESSIONS: PSYCHIC JANE DOHERTY

Holding the sheathed sword tightly with both hands, Jane Doherty began the session by saying, "I am feeling a different energy in each hand. The upper curve of the sword is not pulsating. Yet, the underneath part of the sword is pulsating as if a heart was beating in my hand. I see a lot of blood. And I see an image of someone beheaded with one swoop of this sword."

Jane closed her eyes and after a moment of silence she began to again speak. "I sense that the man who held this sword was not alone when he killed people with it. I see an image of some sort of military people, but I do not think it is a contingency of soldiers. They do not look like the soldiers of today. They give me an impression of ruthless, warrior-type men who enjoyed killing. I can see them cutting grass. It is tall grass and then I see them going off and ... Oh my God! I think they used the sword

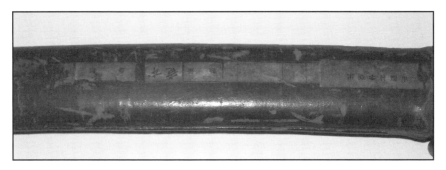

Close-up of the military identification tag that was affixed to an outer side of the sword's sheath. (*Photo Credit – Author's Photo*)

for executions. I see an image of a prisoner standing there and now it looks like someone cuts his head off."

Jane continued, "I get an image of a type of motion (motioning with her hands) that is from side to side and then a downward motion. I don't think you would stab someone with it as it feels more like I'm getting this type of action (motioning) from side to side and downward. It's the way that I'm seeing it in the vision."

At this point I began to interject some thoughts and questions into the session.

Are any names or locations coming through to you?

"I am seeing an image of a jungle area. That is what I don't understand."

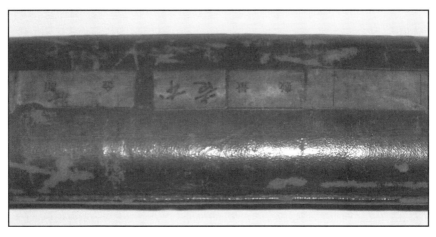

Detail of the military identification tag that was affixed to an outer side of the sword's sheath. (*Photo Credit – Author's Photo*)

I explained to Jane that just about all of the fighting in the Pacific was island related. NCO's, mostly sergeants in the Japanese army, carried this type of weapon.

"Oh! That is definitely the terrain I am seeing. It is more like brush in a jungle area. So that's why I would also be seeing a small group of men, like he would be leading it?"

Exactly, he would have a small group or patrol with him.

As the session continued, I decided to add more information that may help Jane with her psychic receiving by informing her that this was one of the types of weapons that the Japanese would have used without hesitation in the killing of enemy soldiers and civilians alike.

"To me I only feel ruthless, negative energy around the sword. The images I see are only of blood and death. I see soldiers just chopping off heads and limbs. This is so gruesome. I hope I can let go of these images or I will probably have nightmares tonight. I'm trying to think if a name comes up. I'm receiving a name 'Tisu.' or 'Tisui'."

I went on to explain that most of the blades used in these swords were made hundreds of years – dynasties – ago. The only changes that may have taken place would be in changing the tuska (handle) or the tsuba (guard). Connected to them are family and religious connotations.

"That may be, that's why I'm seeing a round gong-like object."

What you are referring to would be something that would have been found in a temple in Japan or on one of the islands that the Japanese occupied during WWII.

"I don't feel that this is surrounded by anything positive. I feel a lot of blood connected to it. I just keep getting this vision of execution."

Yes, they were used quite a bit for executions.

Concluding the session Jane stated, "That's what I see beside the images in the jungle terrain and the large numbers of men; the soldiers just going along a roadway chopping off heads randomly and stabbing bodies."

"You better cleanse the sword. I wouldn't want that hanging around my house. The energy from it is too strong for me to be comfortable."

CHAPTER 40

YOUNG MAN AND HIS ARMBAND

Cloth armband once worn with Arian pride by a member of the Hitler Youth.
(*Photo Credit – Author's Photo*)

F inding sanctuary among my artifacts, this armband lay at rest for many years and only recently was awakened to my detecting of strong latent energy surrounding it.

Old before their time, the Hitler Youth (German: *Hitler-Jugend*, abbreviated HJ) was a paramilitary organization of the Nazi Party. It existed from 1922 to 1945. The HJ was the second oldest paramilitary Nazi group, founded one year after its adult counterpart, the *Stumabteilung* (the SA).

Originally established in 1922 as the *Jungsturm* Adolf Hitler, the HJ was based in Munich, Bavaria. The HJ served to train and recruit future members of the *Stumabteilung* (or "Storm Regiment"), the adult paramilitary wing of the *Nationalsozialistische Deutsche Arbeiterpartei* or NSDAP, the German Nazi Party.

Viewed as future "Aryan supermen," the HJ were indoctrinated in anti-Semitism. One aim was to instill the motivation that would enable HJ members, as soldiers, to fight faithfully for the Third Reich. The HJ put more emphasis on physical and military training than on academic study.

After the Boy Scout movement was banned throughout German-controlled countries, the HJ appropriated many of its activities, though changed in content and intention. For example, many HJ activities closely resembled military training, with weapons training, assault course circuits, and basic stratcgy. Some cruelty by the older boys toward the younger ones was tolerated and even encouraged, since it was believed this would weed out the unfit and harden the rest.

PSYCHIC IMPRESSIONS: PSYCHIC MARYANNE VASNELIS

At first Maryanne began picking up hatred and very clearly the name "Christopher" and began seeing a gun (rifle) with a bayonet attached to it and that it somehow played a part in getting this armband.

Seeing a young person with blond hair and a slightly reddish complexion with small "granny" type round black metal-framed eyeglasses wearing the armband, she could envision someone using the rifle and trying to kill him in close quarters.

"I would say that his age was closer to twenty-four but I keep getting twenty-four to thirty-five. I not certain about the uniform I'm seeing, but I keep seeing three lines or bars attached to one of the arms."

The young man's spirit now entered the scene, conveying to Maryanne that he was not connected to it (the armband) but that it once belonged to him. She interpreted this to mean that he was trying to say that he was not attached to it, like a ghost would be. Maryanne immediately began to feel "goose bumps" about her body!

The reason why the spirit was coming through was simply because he knew that the armband was something that once belonged to him and now Maryanne was given another name, "Henry John," but indicated that she was not certain if this was a full name or a partial one. The spirit indicated that this was the individual who had taken the armband away from him.

"He must not have been twenty-four years of age because he now saying that he died a twenty-five and I'm seeing some sort of explosion." When asked if the spirit was standing next to her she replied, "Not in as much as he is standing here but that his energy is, that he is somewhere else but that he is sending his energy toward us."

I had mentioned to Maryanne that I wished to convey to him that his piece (armband) would be in good hands and well taken care of now. Immediately she informed me that he responded by saying that he was trying to pay back his debt, referring to his part in the war. He had mistaken my reference to the "piece" and took it as the word "peace."

CHAPTER 41

GERMAN NAVAL DAGGER

Once worn with pride and lost in defeat, what weary spirit may still be attached to his beloved dagger? High latent energy surrounds this showpiece dagger that was once the proud possession of a Naval Officer who had held an administrative position somewhere in Third Reich.

PSYCHIC IMPRESSIONS: PSYCHIC JANE DOHERTY

The first question that Psychic Jane Doherty had when first picking up the dagger was, "why did it have an eagle on it?"

Before the session continued, I explained that the majority of German WWII material, badges, daggers, and cloth identification display the eagle as being symbolic, equating with strength.

"I am hearing the name Carl and Von Gusten. Almost immediately Jane asked, where are the naval bases in Europe? Where is Nice located?"

Briefly replying to both of Jane's questions, I mentioned that Germany had a considerable number of Navy bases in France and in Germany proper. A few that came to mind were Kiel, Hamburg, Lübeck, and Wilhelmshaven in Germany and Brest, Nice, and Cherbourg in France.

"Lübeck resonates the most with me. My reaction to that name is different. I have a more connected feeling in my 'gut' to that name than the others. I feel that it is from that base or from near that area. However, I still hear Nice, yet I do not know why. The owner could have traveled to Nice, too, for a trip or side excursion.

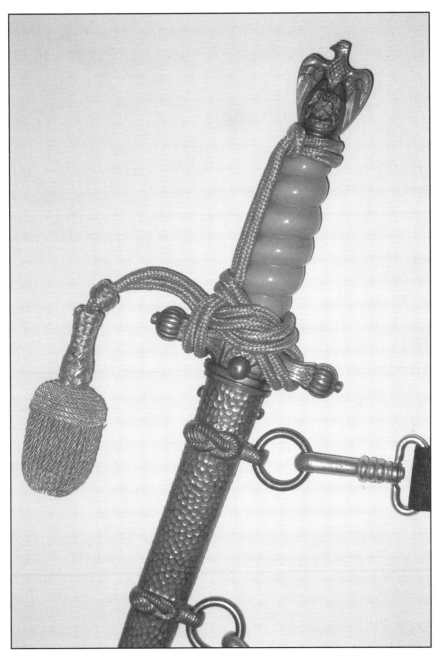

A rare German Naval officer's dress dagger, complete with administrative hangers, that was used by an officer serving in Naval administration. The firm of P.D. Luneschloss – Soligen, produced the dagger. (*Photo Credit – Author's Photo*)

The dagger has a different energy than the other weapons I have held. It feels neutral, without any pulsating or strong energy. Now, of course, I am holding the sheath and not the blade, which could make a difference in my perception."

Jane cautiously removed the dagger from the sheath and immediately sensed energy. "Now I feel a strong pulsating energy emanating from it."

I asked Jane if it was possible that someone may have been stabbed with this dagger.

"No, I do not feel energy at the tip, which is interesting to note. I feel the energy at the base [cross guard]. I interpret that to mean the energy is coming from the owner's body. I think he wore it hanging from his belt. Therefore, I do not feel he killed anyone with it. I also

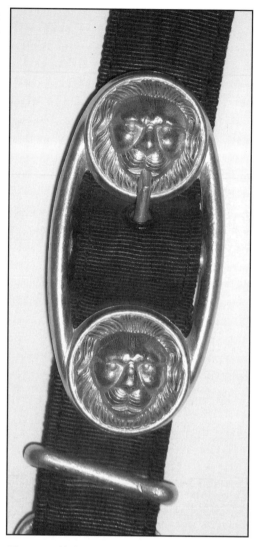

Close-up of the aluminum silver color emblem on the hangers. (*Photo Credit – Author's Photo*)

see a celebration or ceremony. Would they also wear this at some event because I'm getting sort of a celebration, more like a ceremony? I feel that this person who wore this attended many celebrations?"

After explaining to Jane that it was a common practice for German naval officers to attend many ceremonies and various events the session came to an end.

CHAPTER 42

VIVA LA FRANCE

This is a French First World War helmet that was worn during WWII.
(*Photo Credit – Author's Photo*)

T his French helmet was known as the *Casque Adrian* and was introduced just prior to the First World War. The helmet was named in honor of French General August Louis Adrian. First used in 1915, and throughout WWI, this helmet form was sustained in its use by the French military throughout the Second World War as well.

PSYCHIC IMPRESSIONS: PSYCHIC MARYANNE VASNELIS

Maryanne's first impression was receiving the name "France" and that there was some energy as I had detected earlier using my pendulum. Her indication was that this helmet was found in a little town, first northwest and then southwest of Paris and that the town name began with the letter "F."

There was no additional psychic information that came forth from this session; however, as a side note, the only town in France that I was able to locate is the town of Foix. Foix is located in southern France and a little to the southwest in relation to Paris. In 1290, Foix became home to the counts of Bearn. The most dynamic count was Gaston Fébus, who appreciated literature and poetry but also ordered the death of his own brother and son. The counts resisted French rule until 1607 when the area was annexed and fell under the rule of King Henri IV. Beneath the castle you'll find an eleventh-century church and narrow streets lined with medieval, half-timbered houses and a small bronze fountain "de L'Oie" (goose). Foix also boasts the underground river of Labouiche which forms an impressive limestone subterranean gallery.

CHAPTER 43

UNTIL DEATH
DO US PART

Who was this German Wehrmacht warrior that had been stripped of his belt? The strong latent energy surrounding it is an indication that he may still be connected to it. The question is why a simple part of his uniform may be a reason for him not to have crossed over? This is the case concerning many items of clothing, from individual items to complete uniforms. Some spirits will communicate their reasons while others may still be confused as to their circumstances.

This belt and buckle was the standard issue for enlisted personnel of the *Wehrmacht* (Army – German: *Armee*). Some of this type were produced with aluminum buckles having a pebbled finish to the background, while others were produced of steel with a smooth background and finished in a field gray (German: *feldgrau*) paint. What I have presented here is one of the latter types with the buckle still retaining some of its original field gray finish.

PSYCHIC IMPRESSIONS:
PSYCHIC MARYANNE VASNELIS

Maryanne's first vision was seeing a great deal of fighting taking place on land but that the energy she was feeling seemed "cold." "It seemed that the person who possessed this belt had kept it himself for a while and that he had made peace with the war."

The reference here seems to be to the individual who had taken the belt and not the German soldier who originally wore it. The indication was that this person had moved on and that the war

German Wehrmacht soldier's field belt with an unusual twist. (*Photo Credit – Author's Photo*)

was behind him. The feeling was mutual that this reference was to an American soldier.

Continuing with the feeling that this belt was not taken in battle, the impression was that it had been taken from somebody who had died in a hospital. The feeling was that the person who took the belt really did not take it from anyone; that since the German soldier had passed on and that the American soldier was sort of in charge of the personal items, at the time, this was not important enough to send home. Since most of the items had been scheduled for discard, he decided that he would just keep it.

As a side note, uncommon relationships during wartime were formed between members of opposing forces and I can see this scenario happening more so in military hospitals between patients and those caring for them.

160

CHAPTER 44

CONNECTION TO A CONCENTRATION CAMP

This is a letter that was addressed to a member of the Wallisch family, one that has a concentration camp connection to an female former guard.
(*Photo Credit – Author's Photo*)

This envelope and card came from the estate of a former SS-Brigadeführer Hermann Barth. During the Third Reich period, Hermann Barth was a teacher in the SS Education School in Berlin. His connections extended to Reichsführer-der SS Heinrich Himmler, Reichsmarschall Hermann Göring,

Detail. (*Photo Credit – Author's Photo*)

and other high Nazi officials. It seems that he had also known the Wallisch family.

Erna Wallisch, born Erna Pfannenstiel, was the daughter of a postal clerk in eastern Germany in 1922. Wallisch joined the Nazi party when she was still a teenager and became a camp guard at the Ravensbruck women's concentration camp near Berlin. Wallisch later transferred to the Majdanek death camp in Poland, where she was based between October 1942 and January 1944.

In Lublin she had a romance with Georg Wallisch, a Nazi guard, who she later married in March 1944. George Wallisch was related to Generalkonsul Dr. F. Wallisch, to whom the envelope is addressed.

PSYCHIC IMPRESSIONS: PSYCHIC JANE DOHERTY

I prefaced this session with Psychic Jane Doherty by, as I have with the V-Mail letter in another chapter, telling her briefly that it had two connections. The first connection was in the name Wallish and that the second one is a connection to a morbid place.

Jane's only impression was, "It is giving me the creeps! All that I feel with it is death! It almost feels as though death is all around this envelope. Why, I don't know except that it's telling me concentration camp; somebody from there."

CHAPTER 45

PHANTOM OF THE MASK

FROZEN IN TIME

PSYCHIC IMPRESSIONS:
PSYCHIC JANE DOHERTY

Not wishing to try the mask on, Psychic Jane Doherty held it, sandwiched between her two hands. I could not blame her for not wanting to try it on, as the possibility that someone had either died or may have been killed while wearing it existed.

"It makes me feel that this particular mask was worn to hide the individual from being recognized. I get a feeling he wore it to a secret meeting so the person he met could not identify him. He did not trust the person, so this could have been worn by a 'spy'."

I relayed to Jane that I could tell her only that it is a cold weather mask and that I know very little else about it.

"That may be what the mask was intended to be used for, but I receive impressions that the owner wore it for more than just to shield his face from the cold. I feel that it was stolen and used to hide a person's identity. I sense that this person may have been trying to infiltrate an enemy camp. I hear German being spoken. Again, I sense some sort of spy activity."

I explained to Jane that much of the European campaign had been fought during some of the harshest winter months, so her feelings were indeed quite possible. Nothing more had come to

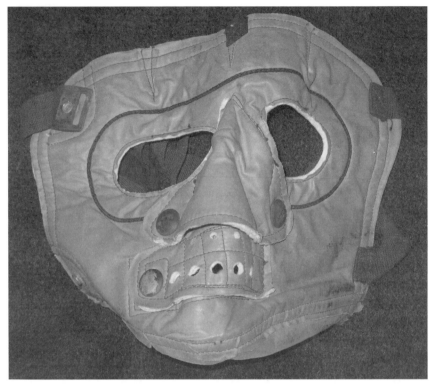

Cold weather mask reveals a paranormal spy drama. (*Photo Credit – Author's Photo*)

Jane; however, I felt that her feelings added some psychic flavor to this artifact and that it may be worthy of additional psychic intervention at another time.

CHAPTER 46

IS THE WAR OVER? CURIOUS SPIRITS WANT TO KNOW

In reading this chapter, you may wonder why I have included it in my book and what the connection is to wartime artifacts. The connection is simply that I participate with my daughter's group, New Jersey Ghost Organization (NJGO) on many significant investigations of historic structures and locations that have direct connections to various wartime periods. My use of the pendulum plays a major part at the start of each of these investigations. I will do an initial walkthrough using it to determine areas where latent energy is present. Next, when one of the group's psychics does their walkthrough, we will compare our results and usually we can correlate the areas or "hot spots." Both the psychic and myself will evaluate any artifacts from the wartime period that may be in the structure while the group is engaged in the equipment setup phase for the investigation.

The Village Inn is a two-story clapboard colonial period structure, located in Englishtown, New Jersey, boasting approximately eleven rooms, an attic, a main staircase, a back spiral staircase, and four fireplaces. Originally, the structure was the home of a tailor shop; it was sold and expanded to accommodate the new owner's large family. It was eventually turned into a tavern/inn by 1766. The location was a stop on the stagecoach line, creating a busy establishment for not only town business, but as a center place during the Revolutionary War, specifically during the pivotal Battle of Monmouth, a battle only

Exterior view of the historical, haunted Village Inn located in Englishtown, New Jersey. General George Washington once trod here during the pivotal Battle of Monmouth during the Revolutionary War. (*Photo Credit – Author's Photo*)

lasting one day from dawn to sunset. This battle was considered the turning point of the Revolutionary War.

Located on the property is a barn and a cold-house where the brew for the patrons of the tavern/inn was kept, along with other perishable items.

General George Washington, later referred to as "The Father of Our Country," resided only a half block from the inn in a period residence and used the inn as his headquarters during the Battle at Monmouth. It was here that Washington drew up the court marshal orders against Major General Charles Lee for his conduct during the Battle at Monmouth, resulting in Lee's arrest and subsequent trial in New Brunswick, New Jersey.

Initially upon arrival, team members were speaking about the Battle of Monmouth and were reading pages from a book found near one of the several display cases, when during their conversation the lights in the bar room began to flicker.

After our two psychics had done their walk-through, team members were split into two groups; one team was assigned the first floor and the other the second floor. While on the second floor, one of the team members witnessed a black figure lean out from the doorway of the last room on the left side of the hallway, just to the left of the main staircase. Lights would also flicker on the second floor during the upstairs team's investigation. Psychic Jane Doherty worked with the second floor team and Psychic Lisa Palandrano worked with the first floor team.

After our psychics Lisa Palandrano, a member of the group who had discovered her psychic gift at the age of twelve, and nationally recognized Psychic Jane Doherty, both present on this investigation, conducted separate walk-throughs. We were able to have a three-way correlation of the hot spots before the actual first phase of the investigation began. The second stage of this investigation was a séance conducted by Psychic Jane Doherty, proving to be very valuable to the investigation.

Interesting facts on Psychic Jane Doherty's "Paranormal Stomach" as quoted from her website. "Doctors cannot give a medical reason for the bizarre expansion of Jane's stomach as she reacts to spirit energy." What happens is that she can feel spirit energy and somehow it connects to her stomach, becoming sensitized to subtle energy fields. If there is paranormal activity in the area the stomach reacts.

During Jane's walk-through a chilling feeling was felt in her stomach as she had felt when she was outside the building seeing a vision of a hanging, the individual hung was a black man, and hearing the names Frederick and Douglass. She followed a path around a table to a doorway leading into the back section inside the building. Once inside, Jane's stomach released and the chilling feeling was gone. Back inside, near a doorway in the bar room area, the lights began to flicker and Jane felt a strong feeling of death. She felt that a stabbing had taken place in the room just above. Also felt was a male presence in front of the dining room door at her right.

Walking into the meeting room, Jane felt chills, her stomach was out, and she walked a path in front of both fireplaces, where previously an electromagnetic field detector, EMF, had recorded a reading of five. Now the meter reacted with a reading of eight as she stopped between the fireplaces, stating that she felt she was back in time. Images of a meeting going on, seeing a gavel hitting the table, and observing there were several men, she saw them running out and hiding. Jane's stomach released after just passing the second fireplace.

As the walk-through continued, Jane stopped at a window in the small hallway just outside of the kitchenette, her stomach reacted, and she felt that there was once a door leading to the outside back of the building where the window now stands.

The reference to the names Frederick and Douglass is believed to be associated with the American abolitionist Frederick Douglass, one of the most influential lecturers and authors in American history. Douglass himself had escaped slavery. Obviously, the man that Psychic Jane Doherty sensed being hung in the Village Inn's yard was not Frederick Douglass. What is believed to have occurred was that the spirit was indeed that of a slave during the 1700s and that was the way he made reference to the circumstances, by referencing a powerful figure in history. Perhaps he was one of the slaves of the homeowner or was simply hiding at the Inn for fear of being captured by the British. Slaves were hidden during the Revolutionary War out of fear of the British taking them for their own. So even though Douglass came almost a century later, it was just a reference.

During Psychic Lisa Palandrano's walk-through, beginning outside the inn, she sensed images of horses with and without carriages coming in and out of the Main Street side of the property near the present gate. She stated that she touched a tree and it said that it had been there longer than the house and that its brothers had been cut down. The main images that she envisioned were horses, not sensing any spirits at that time, but sensing people outside.

Back inside the meeting room, images began to immerge. This room had also been used as an eating room. Psychic Lisa Palandrano was seeing images of large tables but felt no presence. In the hallway, Lisa felt that the wood floors were made from the wood of local trees and as she walked from the hallway into the front dining room and bar area she turned quickly and uttered the word "ale."

Back in the kitchenette, Lisa felt that it had been added on at a later time period and as she peered out the window in the hallway, located just outside the kitchenette, she again saw images of horses and brown chickens. She felt that Indians were here first, seeing images of headdresses.

At this point during the walk-through, Lisa sensed that someone had died of natural causes upstairs as that area was a sleeping area whereas the downstairs was more of a party area. She also had images of "small bones" and questioned if any baby bones were found on the grounds. She had the feeling that many people had passed through here during the inn's longevity, that "important" people had been here, also seeing images of men's top coats with the long style backs. The EMF readings during Lisa's walk-through remained at normal levels.

The séance conducted by Psychic Jane Doherty began after the major session of the investigation wound down and one of the goals was to see if additional evidence might be captured with our equipment and to see if a specific spirit/spirits who remained at this location might be pinpointed.

As the séance got under way the general feeling, almost immediately, was that there were at least two spirits coming through to both Jane and one other team member. The feeling was described as a pressure emanating from above their heads down to their shoulders. There was an overwhelming feeling of sadness overcoming some of the team members, bringing uncontrolled tears to their eyes. One of the team members, feeling the head pressure, also felt a bleeding or seeping sensation as though this member's head was wrapped in some sort of bandage. It also felt webby, like that of a fine spider web on their skin.

At times during the séance lights flickered and all heard the sound of quick, short, light footsteps from the main staircase on the second floor and what seemed to be a knocking emanating from the far corner of the meeting room.

While one of the team members felt a heavy breathing sensation and saw his father's face (his father had passed on when the member was only six months old). He also felt pressure on his lap, as though someone was sitting on it.

One team member experienced the most traumatic sensations of being freezing cold, more sadness, and pain in the back. As the pain became more intense, the member may have blacked out for a few seconds because the next thing that she recalled was that she was actually crying.

In more than one instance team members sitting next to an individual having an experience also felt the experience slightly through the connection made by holding hands. The experiences seemed to have been mimicking what had taken place in this location during the Battle of Monmouth for both soldiers and civilians stayed nearby or at the Inn.

Spirit interaction seems to pop up when you least expect it. During the séance two interactive spirits of Continental Army soldiers were encountered, seemingly in hiding and not aware of their demise. Jane told them that the war was over and that they no longer had the need to be in hiding. One of them asked Jane who had won the war; the Continental Army was her reply. Their reaction seemed to be that of peace, their duty here on this earthly plane was now completed, so Jane proceeded to help them to the light and to cross over. I cannot imagine a more fitting end to this investigation.

PART III

INVESTIGATIVE TECHNIQUES

CHAPTER 47

HOW I INVESTIGATE ARTIFACTS

There is really no secret to investigating artifacts; simple equipment will work just fine. How sophisticated you wish to make it is up to you, but I like to do my investigating with minimal confusion. It makes any evidence obtained easier to either confirm or to seek out a logical, alternate explanation.

The first thing that I look for in any artifact is whether latent energy is in some way connected to it. How this is accomplished is by using my pendulum. This is really the simplest step, but a very necessary one. Next, I will prepare the artifact for photographing. When photographing artifacts I always try to use a tripod to eliminate the possibility of camera shake. However, this is not always possible, especially when visiting museums, as most do not permit the use of tripods for safety reasons. The tripod is an especially useful piece of equipment should you not be using the camera's built in flash. In a separate chapter I will talk of the advantages of photographing an artifact in total darkness, without the use of a flash, by using longer exposures. Film cameras can also be used in this manner. Keep in mind that if you are using a throwaway type camera, you may not be able to get very close to small artifacts. You risk obtaining blurred or out of focus images if you try.

My preference is to work in a quiet room, usually in the evening. I use a Digital Concepts PS-101™ portable light studio. The studio consists of a light box, two high output lights, a mini tripod and a built in carrying case that is only slightly larger that a large attaché case, making it very portable. It has two built in, non-reflective white and black backgrounds and is very simple to use and obtain shadow-less photographs of just about anything that you can fit into it. It works with the two tungsten lamps, one on each side of the light box facing the cloth diffusion screens, which are the sides of the box, coupled with the flash of the camera you are using. This setup can also be used with film and video cameras.

You can use a stool or a table to place the artifact on. My suggestion would be to still use non-reflective backgrounds, white, black or medium gray depending on the type of artifact you're photographing. Plain cloth, construction paper or felt squares can be used as background material. First place the non-reflective background on the chair, stool or table and then carefully position the artifact on the background. Using this setup the camera flash is sufficient to record an image for your records.

After making a photographic record of an artifact, I send the photographs, via email, to two of my psychics for their initial impressions. Depending on what information I receive from the psychics I will, in many cases, arrange for a hands on reading by either or both psychics, or by a third psychic.

Armed with the psychic impressions, I will next place a voice recorder, using an external microphone, with the actual artifact and attempt to capture EVP (Electronic Voice Phenomena). This may be done at the time you are initially taking photographs of the artifact or at a later time. However, my preference is doing this at a later time. I have dedicated a separate chapter to describing this technique.

You may wish to consider playing period music while working with an artifact. Now, you may be wondering exactly what this would accomplish. I use period music as a tool, not only to attract the spirit or spirits who may be associated with the artifact but also as method of placing them more at ease, increasing the possibility of a manifestation in some form. I only use this during the photographic phase of the investigation, but not during the EVP phase. In short, playing period music acts in a similar manner to that of white noise.

Another factor that you may wish to consider is the surroundings in which you will be working with your artifacts. I may have a slight advantage in that my home was constructed in 1940 and the architecture inside and out reflects the style of the wartime period. In short, your surroundings can play an important part in the results that you obtain when investigating artifacts from any time period.

CHAPTER 48

PREPARING TO TAKE PHOTOGRAPHS

The most important factor is keeping your camera ready and by this I mean that fresh or recharged batteries should be in it at all times, film in a film camera, carrying extra sets of batteries when going to a location, and should you be using a film camera an extra supply of film is a must. I'm certain that most of you check your equipment and supplies beforehand, yet I find that some don't. That is my reason for saying this in the beginning of this chapter, to stress its importance.

A common belief that spirit presences drain energy from batteries may in all probability be true, as they utilize energy from many sources. However, battery draining may occur whether they are in the camera or not, so always make certain that you have several sets of fresh or recharged batteries with you. In most modern cameras, film and digital, the electronics and the energy within them, play a part in attracting a spirit to sap the energy, expediting the premature drainage of batteries. This applies to other electronic devices that you may be using as well.

Most commonly used cameras today are digital, offering not only flexibility, but also the ability to view your results immediately after taking a picture. Setting the camera in the automatic mode takes the technical thinking out of picture making. However, this may not always be desirable, so read your camera instruction booklet carefully, as you may, depending upon the situation, wish to consider switching to a manual mode.

Most digital cameras operate in a limited infrared spectrum. This infrared capability is built into most digital cameras in use today and it is my belief this accounts for the larger amount of orbs photographed in recent years. If you want to test this with your camera, take your TV remote and point it at yourself, press the on button and you will not see the light bulb in the tip of the remote light up because it is an infrared light source. When you view the remote while pressing the on button through your digital camera's LCD screen or take a photo of it, you will see the light is illuminated. This indicates that your digital camera can pick up and record infrared light. When you take a photograph with your digital camera, you may actually be capturing images in both the visible and infrared light spectrums. Since the common belief is that anomalies rely on energy to manifest and that a portion of this energy exists within the infrared spectrum, using digital cameras will give you a better tool and a better chance of capturing an anomaly.

Auto focus can be a bit tricky, especially when taking pictures through glass frames or glass windowed display cases. Always be aware of the fact that, although transparent, glass also has a solid surface. The impulse or beam that the auto focus of the camera emits must hit and reflect back, enabling proper focusing. If you attempt to takc a picture through a glass window, standing directly in front of the window may produce out of focus results. Try standing at a slight angle to the window's surface, usually at approximately a thirty-degree angle.

Reflections caused by the camera's flash and other objects can be very misleading as spirit presences are not reflective as solid objects are, and spirit presences do not depend on light to make themselves known and will record on digital, film or video regardless. Energy gathered from the flash illumination or other instruments may intensify the reactions of a spirit in being able to manifest itself.

Take your time and hold your camera as steady as possible. Camera movement (shake) in combination with auto focus is a prime concern that cannot be overlooked. Keep in mind that with a camera set on full automatic, the exposure is being completely controlled by the electronics of the camera, according to the conditions. Although this is accomplished almost instantaneously, certain conditions may dictate slower shutter speeds to the camera, in which case even the slightest movement of hand or subject will be recorded.

The same basic principles apply when using film cameras (the most common are 35mm cameras). I have found that the fully manual 35mm camera is the better choice. A minimum of four hundred-speed film or faster is recommended, keeping in mind that the faster the film speed, the greater possibility that grain will be present. Both camera, film, and cassette light leaks are always a possibility, along with chemical processing errors; all can affect your end results.

Polaroid cameras are another option. If you do decide to use Polaroid, the possibility of analyzing your results may become a bit simpler, as retouching of a Polaroid print can easily be detected and your concerns that normally accompany digital photographs can be eliminated. You may also wish to try using black and white as opposed to color film, mainly due to the fact that the tonal range of black and white is greater (black to white with subtle gray tones between). Your chance of picking up a faint anomaly is greatly increased with the use of black and white film. The only negative aspect when using black and white film is being able to locate a processing facility. On a positive note, you can set yourself up to process black and white film in your home at a moderate expense with used equipment. The processing chemicals are still readily available.

One important factor that should not be overlooked is that you need to beware of your surroundings. Look for areas or items that may cause reflections if you are using flash or from ambient light in the environment, such as window light when photographing interiors during daylight hours, or light from outside sources at night. Interior home lighting from lamps, candles, glassware setting on tables, in glass cabinets, metal framed pictures and other shinny surfaces, television screens, windows, mirrors, etc.

In summary, don't complicate things; you are your best source for drawing a spirit presence. Know your equipment and, when viewing your end results, do so by process of elimination of what it may not be. In the end you may have something positive, a paranormal anomaly.

CHAPTER 49

CAPTURING ELECTRONIC VOICE PHENOMENON - EVP

After a long conversation with Todd M. Bates, creator of Haunted Voices, utilizing his expertise in the area of EVP and the technical aspects for analyzing, I have developed the following protocol. There is absolutely no difference in using this protocol when working with an artifact or on other investigations. This protocol can apply when using either digital (with some exceptions) or analog voice recorders.

EQUIPMENT

You can use one voice recorder or multiple recorders. It is suggested that, if you use multiple voice recorders, you may wish to standardize by using one make and model voice recorder.

Whatever your choice of batteries is, you may wish to consider standardizing with those as well.

Standardize the type and make of microphone.

The positive aspect of standardizing is that you only have to learn the operation of one voice recorder and it lessens the possibility of recording false positives due to the differences in equipment.

However, you may still encounter differences in the performance of like equipment, but the chances are less.

RECORDING USING ANALOG CASSETTES

It is most important to record on one side of a cassette fully at each location. Never re-record over a previously recorded cassette. The reason for this is that you want to avoid picking up voice residue from the previous recording. The brand of cassettes is your choice but they should be of the "normal bias" type. If you are using multiple recorders, it is recommended that you use the same brand of cassette in each voice recorder.

PRELUDE TO PARANORMAL

When you first arrive at the location, do a walk-around with the person of the location only. Let the individual describe each room (living room, bathroom, etc.) as you proceed through the location. Ask the individual if any unusual activity has occurred in this location. Repeat this procedure in each room. It is important to keep your recorder running throughout the entire walk through.

PLACEMENT OF VOICE RECORDERS

When using only one voice recorder, place it in one location and let it run for the entire time for one complete side of the cassette (this only applies to analog voice recorders). When placing voice recorders in multiple locations, the same applies.

When the time has elapsed for the first side of the cassette, the recorder/recorders will automatically turn off (not applicable with digital voice recorders). Digital recorders will only turn off when a file is full. With digital voice recorders you will have to time each session yourself.

When using an external microphone (which is recommended) place it at its maximum distance from the voice recorder's location. Microphones should be cushioned if possible when placed on a hard surface (dresser, table, floor, etc.) to lessen the possibility of picking up vibrations. If possible, you should cushion the voice recorder as well, especially when you are using the built in microphone only (not recommended).

When you leave the room, close the door. Only you should enter the location if necessary during the recording session and when the session is completed. No one else should be permitted to enter during or immediately after until you clear the room. If at all possible, you may wish to seal off the location during the recording session. This may not always be possible.

Should you decide to record another session in the same room, flip the cassette and repeat the procedure above.

SUGGESTIONS FOR OBTAINING POSITIVE RESULTS

The recommended investigative hours are between midnight and six a.m. The ideal hours are from two a.m. to four a.m. The peak or witch hour is three a.m. After midnight is when the outside atmospheric conditions begin to change, allowing for increased static and when what is commonly termed the "veil" becomes thinner, making it easier for spirit activity to react.

You can double your chances for positive results when recording EVP in a specific location by placing a video camera in the same room, using night vision. Simply set up the camera and turn it on, saying nothing of what it is or does. The spirit/ spirits may wonder where the extra energy is coming from and they will use it to increase their vocal ability or to manifest in some form, unaware that they are being videotaped. Unlike the video recorder, discuss the voice recorder with any presences that you feel are in the room, telling them what the device is and what it does. Hold it up to show them before placing it in the location that you feel is appropriate. Make certain that the angle of view of the video camera will be picking up the recorder. If you wish, you can also place an electro magnetic field detector, EMF, within view so that the camera can pick up any disruption that may be crossing its path as additional back up evidence.

By leaving the video camera running, you will also be recording voice. With Hi-8 video cameras, the voice is digitized, which will result in an extremely clear recording. You may be surprised when you view the videotape; you may actually pick up an anomaly since the spirit/spirits are not aware that they are being recorded and have picked up the extra energy.

You may wish to consider the use a spongy, foam material to cushion your voice recorder. By doing so, you will lessen the chance of picking up vibrations if it is placed on a hard surface, such as a table, dresser or on the floor. It is also advisable as well to cushion an external microphone, if you're using one, for the same reasons.

Digital voice recorders, when left unattended in a location, will record their best when standing in an upright position. This is simply due to the internal microphone being omni directional. For this purpose, you can use two pieces of foam rubber, cutting a slot in the upper piece to accommodate the recorder. By gluing the two pieces together, the bottom piece forming a base for the recorder to rest on, you will be allowing the recorder to safely stand in an upright position.

WHITE NOISE

With the blockbuster movie that came out in January of 2005, the term white noise was viewed in a different light and for a different purpose than that for which paranormal investigators actually use it. White noise, to a paranormal investigator, is a type of sound that is produced by combining a lot of different frequencies together. If you took all of the imaginable tones that a human can hear and combined them together, you would have white noise.

The description "white" describes this type of noise in the same way it describes white light. The word "white" is used because the color white is created when all the colors in the light spectrum combine. A prism can be used to separate white light back into its component colors. White noise (also called white sound) is a combination of equal amounts of different frequencies of sound, just like white light is a combination of colors. You can think of white noise as 20,000 tones all playing at the same time and at the same level. Because white noise contains so many frequencies, it is often used to mask other sounds. If you are in a motel and voices from the room next door are leaking into your room, you might turn on the fan to drown out the voices. The fan produces a good approximation of white noise. Why does that work? Why does white noise drown out voices?

An example of how white noise works with the brain is this: Say you just parked your car at a mall with your two friends in the back seat and your cell phone rings. You pick it up and start talking. While you are talking to the person on the phone one of your friends in the car starts asking you a question. Normally you would either stop listening to the person on the phone for a minute, or you would hold up your hand and ask the person in the car to wait. Why do we do this? It is because the human brain can actually only listen, process, and understand one voice at a time. If you were to stay on the phone and the two others in the car start talking to each other, you would "hear" them all, but you could only listen to one at a time. Now, to step this up to explaining white noise, let's have the three people in the car walk into the mall. You are still on your cell phone and the other two are still talking. But, as you enter the mall, even they tend to be drowned out. There are simply too many people talking at once. Even if you were to get off of the phone and just sit in say … the food court of the mall, all the noise would be hitting you, but you could still only pick out one conversation to listen to at a time. When we go back to the motel scenario, we can now understand why the fan drowns out the voices coming through the wall. The fan would be like the mall noise, while the voices next door would be the two other people talking as you enter the mall. They are simply lost in the other noise.

The thought that white noise attracts spirits is controversial. It totally depends on which investigator you talk to about it, as their views on the subject differ. Some do not choose to use white noise due to the background it creates for the recording or because they think that it masks over the actual E.V.P. Others swear by it, while still others only use it sometimes. For the same reason some dislike the use of white noise, others like it. One of the positive things about using white noise is that it gives you a constant background noise. This helps to make your recording more credible if you do capture an E.V.P., as it makes it harder to fake one while keeping the background noise unbroken. But I'm getting ahead of myself now. I'm sure your wondering how white noise is used and why. Right? Well, this is where that facts concerning what white noise is start to blur with why it is used, as white noise in relation to the paranormal is all theory ... just like everything else in the paranormal field.

White noise is used as a "base" for recording during E.V.P. sessions. When it is used, it should be played at a very low "hum" in the background. One of the leading theories in relation to the use of white noise is that it "attracts" spirits, therefore getting more EVP's. I have heard of more than one person/group who have tried this and then swear they will never go without it. You may also want to play this in the background while you conduct your investigations. Some feel this helps keep the spirit interested as well as making it easier for them to communicate with you. I recommend you experiment with this process and try different approaches. Find what works for you.

White noise is generated through controlled, various pitches of static that have been previously recorded onto a CD or tape and played at a very low volume. It can interfere with the ability to hear spirit voices but during analysis of a voice recording it can easily be determined at a fixed Hz or Hertz unit frequency (of change in state or cycle in a sound wave, alternating current, or other cyclical waveform) of one cycle per second. When a voice or sound falls between specific Hz, it is considered to be within the normal human hearing range and outside that range, below or above, it is considered to be paranormal.

CHAPTER 50

ELECTRONIC VOICE PHENOMENA - OTHERWISE KNOWN AS E.V.P. -

TODD M. BATES, FOUNDER OF HAUNTED VOICES AND HVRN CORPORATION PARANORMAL TALK RADIO

The mystery of Electronic Voice Phenomena has been around for many years. There are quite a few paranormal investigators out there that refuse to work with the phenomena due to its complications. I personally feel that it is very much worth the extra effort.

EVP is a great communication tool for the other side and the phenomena itself can answer some of the questions that we have all asked ourselves over the years. Simply put, it just makes sense to experiment with E.V.P. during your investigations. It is not at all difficult to capture these voices from the other side. It takes very little knowledge and equipment to do so. There are too many investigators out there who are or feel intimidated by this phenomenon. Many do not take the time to research or educate themselves or their group(s) on the subject. This is one reason why I choose to volunteer my time and services to anyone who wants to learn about this field. I will not go into that right now because this isn't information about ME but for YOU, the investigator, to perhaps learn from and use for your future investigations. I will try and touch on a brief history, some current theories about this topic, a few tips to help you on your way, and still throw my own two cents in.

Thomas A. Edison was the first to look into electronic voice phenomena in the early 1920s. After his mother had been sick for some time, nearing death's door, he decided to try and find a way to communicate with her after she passed. Shortly after he started work his mother did pass on, leaving Thomas with a more urgent need to find a device with his assistant Dr. Miller Hutchison, which was later to be called the Thomas Edison Communicator or TEC. Edison didn't get to complete his work before his own death in 1931. Since that time it has been completed by others using his notes and is being experimented with today. This device is basically like a giant microphone for the dead. It seems to be able to pick out their voices from the air. Very little is known about how this device actually works. These may be available in the future, but I'm certain that they will not come at a low cost. One could only hope that Mr. Edison is very proud that his invention is finally completed, even though he wasn't able to use it himself to communicate with his mother as he intended.

Perhaps my favorite EVP mentor is the now deceased Swedish film producer, Friedrich Juergenson. He captured the phenomena without even knowing it while trying to record bird songs. This was an accident that changed the paranormal arena forever. When Juergenson played the bird songs back, he discovered that he had recorded voices from the other side. Phrases such as "bird voices in the night" and even his own mother, who was then already deceased, contacted him by saying, "Fredrich, you are being watched," "Friedel, my little Friedel can you hear me?" This of course amazed as well as relieved Juergenson. He then began a recording frenzy to try and get in touch with his mother and all other spirits. He died in 1964, but not before he had contacted and confirmed life after death. He was given the title posthumously of, "The Father of E.V.P."

I am sure you are asking, Ok, so what is EVP? Well, I really wish the answer were so simple and easy to explain. Of course, then it wouldn't be called the "unknown." Let me first tell you that there are quite a few theories on how the phenomenon actually occurs. Some believe that the spirit itself simply walks up to the microphone or recording device and speaks into it. I personally find this very hard to believe. How could a spirit that is composed of pure energy, as far as we know, simply speak without vocal cords? The theory that I tend to go with is that the spirit somehow imprints its "magnetic image" onto the recording device. Now, there are some who believe that a "residual" effect takes place when some of the energy that is stored in the area of the known haunting is released. This is very possible and I feel that such objects, like limestone, can hold this kind of energy for long periods of time. I also think that if you are at the right place at the right time, you may just capture some voices of the past.

The Catacombs, located in Paris, France, are a great example of how this may occur. There are thousands of corpses located beneath the streets of Paris and they are far from being at rest. This energy could very well be stored in the actual limestone walls of the catacombs. Residual energy, by the way, is spirit energy that is constantly replaying over time and not an interactive ghost. Another popular theory is that the spirit will speak to us using telepathy or use our own voice and resources to break the communication barrier from their world to ours. After you have experimented with electronic voice phenomena, gaining more knowledge and experience, then perhaps you may come up with your own opinions on this subject. The key is to not be afraid or intimidated by the spirits, but to respect and learn from them.

Secondly, E.V.P. can be captured in a few different ways. There is really no right or wrong way to do it. Numerous groups and investigators claim that their way is the best or the only way to capture E.V.P. I have found that this is completely incorrect and if there were an "expert" in this field then we all could put our equipment away because it would no longer be considered the "unknown." No one knows all of the answers and those that claim they do, need to turn to another avenue to pursue or take this one more seriously.

You can use a standard cassette or digital recording device; however, in my opinion, it is hard to compare with the ancient and bulky Reel-to-Reel recorder. This recorder is what started it all, though it has both its good and bad points. I don't really want to get too technical here so if you would like to read more about the Reel-to-Reel recorder, you can do a simple search for information on the Internet.

When I go on investigations I choose to use both the cassette and digital recorder as I feel they both back each other up. I will caution that you should be sure to use an external microphone with your cassette recorder, not to help hear the spirit better but to reduce the possibility of wheel noise generated by the recorders internal parts. I personally do not use an external microphone with my digital recorder because I feel that the internal mechanisms are not loud enough to disrupt the recording. However, you may have a preference choosing one if you wish.

Many questions have been asked as to what type of tapes should one use in my cassette recorder? Well, the answer is "try them all." If you plan on or know how to use audio editing software in your computer then this really doesn't matter. Some feel that the metal content in the tape helps and it is very possible that it may but for those of us on a strict budget this could get quite costly. I have heard some outstanding E.V.P. captured on "Dollar Store" brand cassette tapes, so that was proof enough for me. Sure, you have the background hiss with these tapes but this can be reduced and cleaned with the computer software, if used.

If you use some common sense and some general knowledge of electronic voice phenomena, then you should have no problem capturing your own E.V.P. I do hope this helps some of you and I cannot stress enough for all of you to give it a try; you just might be surprised at what you record!

CHAPTER 51

EXPERIMENTAL NOISE WITH EVP RECORDING -

TODD M. BATES, FOUNDER OF HAUNTED VOICES

WHITE NOISE - PINK NOISE - CHROME NOISE AND MORE!

We have all heard of different noises that may play a key role in your EVP recordings. This educational article isn't intended to make you believe or disbelieve. What you will read are personal accounts as well as documented experimentation in known haunted areas that coincide with the noises themselves. You can be the judge.

My use of experimental noise all started one day when the two words "white noise" came across my work with software. I was very interested in this noise and learning that it contained every audible sound known to the human ear and beyond just made me even more curious. I found that this noise wasn't very "soothing" at all; I found it rather irritating. I had to find out if it had any positive potential with my EVP research. Some will call this noise a "mask" of deception, and it can be if not used in the proper way, but is there a proper way to use it? This is something we simply do not know, and the sharing of research in the paranormal community is unfortunately uncommon.

We should look much deeper into the use of these noises. Here we will discuss some true accounts and describe some of the experimental noise created by our very own staff at the HVRN Corporation. Keep in mind that these are my personal opinions and accounts and I have been told by many to keep my opinions out of the equation. I strongly choose not to do this, as this is what increases our knowledge and helps us to form our own opinions. To be honest, I have been cut to the bone and ridiculed just for using them and, sure, it used to have an effect on me. However, I have moved on, and that is the basis for this writing.

We have a lot of content to cover, so let's begin with the question, "Why should we try using experimental noises?" We truly don't know if they will work or if these sounds are just a waste of our time. Personally, I would rather be safe than sorry. I started using the experimental noises about three years ago and have had very good results as well as my share of time wasted. I have found in my research that it is best to use them before you even start your recording as it may interfere with the pristine recording you are after, and it could create a large mess if you attempt to analyze your recording later. The first documented time I began using the noises to aid in EVP capture was at a very well known location popularly called "The Sallie House." Some of you may have seen this on television and thought of it as a place of demons and violence. I won't go that far with it but will say that the location has exhibited violent energies. Our Research and Development team made a special trip to this location and our findings (using experimental noises) were great! We simply couldn't get enough of them and just had to try every single noise that our staff created to see its potential first hand. After having a team meeting, we decided to try the softest sounds and work our way to the worst, most erratic of the noises.

Upon doing this we found that the activity actually increased in the home and this was done with no recorders even running at the time. This was an experiment for "physical" activity, not just EVP. Our first noise was a very calm black light humming noise and this seemed very soothing to the ears. We felt it would be the same for the spirits within the home as well. During its thirty-minute experiment period we didn't notice any signs of physical activity, but did notice that we were all very calm and at ease in the home – something that didn't come easy at all.

After its use, we analyzed all of the data and found no evidence of activity in the room where it was introduced. Keep in mind that we used all of the bedrooms upstairs for these experiments, and additionally had some hardware intervention in different locations throughout the home (but not always at the same time.) The upstairs bedrooms were perfect for experiments as they were extremely quiet and very secure because there was only one way upstairs and this decreased the possibility of tampering. We all sat downstairs at our post and monitored different rooms with video equipment as well as a few other devices to aid us in our search for activity. Before each noise was introduced into the environment we would speak aloud our intentions to any spirits present as well as into our dictation devices. We would then take the normal base readings of the area that you would take during any investigation. We would also do EMF and temperature sweeps prior to introducing the noise. After expelling each noise we found one that actually was a key to that particular area as well as one that sparked activity. The noise of choice for this area was "pink noise." This noise contains less than half of the octave of "white noise" and worked very well for the job at hand.

During the thirty minute experiment with this noise we saw not only the atmosphere change into a "thick and difficult to breathe environment" but the physical activity became apparent as well. We began to hear footsteps walking up and down the stairs and what is described as "phantom furniture" sounds in the upstairs spare bedroom. It sounded as if boxes and other slightly heavier objects were being moved around upstairs and we sat there listening and visually observing our surroundings. Finally after many trials we seemed to have found a noise that actually worked. Or was this just because we had played all of the others as well and with the combination it somehow caused a reaction? This we may never know but nonetheless we were on to something.

I have since used the "pink noise" in many other locations and found it to be very useful, as it is less irritating to both the researcher and perhaps even the spirit you are attempting to communicate with. The last time I used this particular noise was at an old theatre that is very active. It really seemed to spark activity as well as give the spirits some kind of avenue to speak through.

In closing, I am not suggesting that these noises work or do not work, but I recommend at least giving them a try to see for yourself. You may discover a few things that would have normally been left behind, or not even noticed at all. I am aware that some say these noises can allow you to do what is called "matrixing" or hearing things that are not really there, but we used these in controlled settings. And in the case of the theatre, we were not even in the area to hear the noise during its introduction. Basically you simply cannot accurately judge it unless you try it. Do not simply listen to what others say, try it for yourself as you may be surprised with the outcome. Try all of the noises and noise combinations. In this way, you can hope to find out if there is any truth to these noises or if it is just all in our heads.

For more information or just for your feedback and comments about the experimental noises, please feel free to contact me via email at toddbates@hauntedvoices.com and I will be more than happy to explain or answer any questions you may have.

CHAPTER 52

RELATED VIEWS

When asked about communicating with spirits and the possible complications that may be involved with an artifact, I recommend keeping it simple, concise, and to the point. Psychic Jane Doherty responded by stating, "It would be very, very difficult to communicate with a spirit in words, considering that the language barrier would have nothing to do with it, as more often than not they will speak in pictures. However, there are times when you would

Author working closely with Psychic Jane Doherty as she evaluates an artifact.
(*Photo Credit – Karen E. Timper, NJGO*)

have communication where a spirit would speak his name; you would have communication in symbol. In my work in doing séances people want to contact many crazy things and it's not going to happen. I have had media contact requesting me to do a séance to contact some well-known personalities and I wouldn't do it. It would be different if you went to the house they lived in, as I had done something involving the late Grace Kelly for television on the "Dead Famous" but I was in a place that she had lived in. To do a séance on a TV stage setting, trying to make contact with some famous personality, there's no way that I would ever do this and I've turned down many requests like that."

EPILOGUE

E xactly how does one bring a book about a never-ending arena of investigation within the endlessly flexible, always shifting, paranormal fabric to time to a close? The paranormal infrastructure is so unique within itself that one can only marvel with its complex nature, as our short span in this realm dictates. I am comfortable in the thought that one day I, as well as you, shall continue to be a part of its vastness after playing out our roles in this earthly theater from our beginning to our destiny.

As I add the final period to my writing I wish to thank you all for reading my book. It is my sincere hope that this book has encouraged many to view artifacts and the spirits who may be connected to them with the kindness and respect they deserve.

Paranormally Yours,

Richard J. Kimmel